CHINESE GRAPHIC DESIGN IN THE TWENTIETH CENTURY

D0914199

CHINESE GRAPHIC DESIGN IN THE TWENTIETH CENTURY

Scott Minick and Jiao Ping

with 285 illustrations, 150 in colour

Thames and Hudson

Opposite: *Street scene in a provincial city, with shop sign and Guomindang banners and flags, late 1930s.*

Wherever possible, captions include title of work; date; author; designer/illustrator/artist; publisher; size in centimetres, height before width. However, complete information has not always survived. Unless otherwise stated, the media are book or magazine covers or illustrations.

Text set in Linotype Weiss

Printed and bound in Singapore by C. S. Graphics Pte Ltd.

目录
Contents

引言

Preface

8

一

1

Chinese Traditions

11

二

2

May Fourth and the
Formative Years

21

三

3

The Shanghai Style

35

四

4

The Progressive Movement

55

五

5

Proletarians and Paper Tigers

73

六

6

Yan'an and the Artistic Ideal

89

七

7

The Revolutionary Machine

101

八

8

The Turbulent Years

119

九

9

Open Doors and Beyond

131

参考要目

Reference Guide

152

Chinese Publishers 152

Select Bibliography 153

Chinese Bibliography 154

Designer Index 155

General Index 158

Preface

Left home young and returned old,
Speaking as then, but with hair grown thin,
And my children meeting me do not know me,
they smile and say, 'Stranger, where do you come from?'
He Zhi-zhang, AD 659–744

Little concern has been given to documenting, much less saving, examples of China's long design history. A great many of the books and magazines illustrated here remain in public circulation in China, but are regarded solely for the value of the written word. When these materials can no longer hold up to the rigours of public use they will be discarded. The speed at which such aesthetically significant materials are being lost is alarming. As China lunges forward in an attempt to modernize, it is routinely disposing of many fine examples of its cultural heritage, much of which is unrecoverable.

If through this book we can preserve at least a portion of China's rich design past, while helping to dispel some of the myths that have kept the country isolated and misunderstood well into the twilight of the 20th century, we will feel that our work has been successful. True to the function of good design, the natural vitality and excitement of the images illustrated here transcend the obstacle of language. Amazingly fresh and full of expression, these materials have managed to survive innumerable upheavals. Through natural catastrophes, wars and political purges they have endured a long and often painful history. It is our hope that this book will serve as a testament not only to the strength and significance of this long record of artistic achievement but to the ongoing spirit of creativity and devotion that has produced it.

I am indebted to many people without whose help this project would have been an impossibility. First and foremost is my wife, Jiao Ping. So much of what I have learned and written about Chinese design has first passed through her. Had it not been for her patience and trust in opening her country to my eyes, this project could not have succeeded.

Together we would also like to thank the following individuals for their support and assistance in collecting valuable information and materials: Mr Qian Jun-tao; Mr Xu Bai-yi; Mr Ren Yi; Mr Wu Qing-yun; Mr Ye Xin and Ms Wu Duan-duan; Ms Cecile Vidaux and the Bibliothèque Municipale de Lyon; Ms Jacqueline Hassan and the Centre de Chine, Paris; Yu Bing-nan and Beijing's Central Academy of Art and Design; Kosima Weber Liu for her help with photographic research; the staff of Thames and Hudson; and finally, the people of China, whose culture continues to produce artists and designers of exceptional merit and in whose hands this history remains.

Scott Minick
Paris, January 1990

1 · Chinese Traditions

Thirty spokes unite in one nave,
And because of the part where nothing exists we have the use of a carriage wheel.
Clay is moulded into vessels,
And because of the space where nothing exists we are able to use them as vessels.
Doors and windows are cut in the walls of a house,
And because they are empty spaces, we are able to use them.
Therefore, on the one hand we have the benefit of existence, and on the other,
we make use of non-existence.

Lao Tzu, *Tao-te ching*, 6th century BC

Above: *Designs containing the eight trigrams of the I Ching and, in the centre, the yin-yang symbol.*

Opposite: *Food vendors, overseen by painted wall graphics designed to educate the public in hygiene and civic law, late 1930s.*

The whole of Chinese art, life and civilization has by tradition been inextricably linked to the concept of harmony; it is through this universal order that all relationships are formed. In the most precious of writings, *The Book of Changes*, relationships are defined as being in a constant state of flux. Only through the *yin* and *yang* principle, which unifies both opposing and complementary forces, is creation given balance. The same may be said within the discipline of Chinese design. There exists in the examples from each period an interplay of existence and non-existence, which is a fundamental basis for their being. For this reason it might be suggested that Chinese design strives for a completeness that transcends the physical expression itself. Each physical component, emotional expression or intellectual consideration must be balanced and unified by its respect for a greater artistic and spiritual harmony.

While many of the designs collected here illustrate a fascination with the interplay of positive and negative space, it is not on this basis that a Chinese design has developed. By contrast to Western design, where the emphasis is more often on positive form to express that which is material, Chinese design traditionally emphasizes the absence of form in an attempt to stress the spiritual. It is, in fact, through this absence of form in a Chinese work that the design is said to be revealed. Similarly, the relative success of a work of art or a design might also be measured in more abstract terms. Frequent reference is made to the *qi*, literally 'air' or spirit, transmitted through the work. A work that lacks this sense is considered incomplete.

Such concern for wholeness in design is deeply rooted in the Confucian conception of the artist-scholar. The Confucian tradition defined artistic excellence through the mastery of poetry, music, calligraphy and painting. Thus no claim to artistry could be successful without a studied knowledge and highly developed ability in each of these areas. It was thought that only by such means could an individual grasp the interrelatedness of things and ultimately approach an understanding of universal harmony and order. With this in mind we can more fully appreciate the intrinsic pervasiveness of design in Chinese society. It is also the key by which the Chinese designer develops a broad interdisciplinary understanding of the design process and is able to form a strong and unifying link between concept and creation.

In a culture that was preeminently literary, expressive graphic works and calligraphy brought the highest artistic recognition, for they most closely paralleled the written word. Therefore it is not surprising to learn that the Chinese first developed the techniques of papermaking, block printing and movable typography.

The actual invention of paper as we know it originated in China during the first century AD, but its manufacture remained a carefully guarded secret. Knowledge of the methods for its production were only discovered in AD 751 when a group of skilled Chinese papermakers was captured in Samarkand in Central Asia by Arab traders plying the Silk Road. From this encounter the techniques were introduced to the Moorish regions of Spain in 1150 and

Two views of the early papermaking process. A finely woven screen is lifted from the vat of paper pulp (left), allowing a thin layer to form before it is applied to the sides of a wood-fired kiln for drying (right).

The earliest surviving Chinese woodcut – the Diamond Sutra, AD 868.

shortly after spread throughout the rest of Europe. Papermills were thus established in France in 1189, in Italy in 1276 and in Germany in 1391.

The earliest varieties of Chinese paper date from the Western Han dynasty (206 BC–AD 8) and were made from a combination of bamboo fibres and silk. Such formulas proved to be both expensive and heavy and by the period of the Eastern Han dynasty (AD 25–220) a less expensive and more practical method was in use. The refinement of paper ingredients is credited to Cai Lun (d. AD 121), who came from what is now Hunan Province. During the period of Emperor He Di, Cai Lun served as an official in charge of producing decorative objects for the Emperor's use. By c. AD 114 Cai Lun had risen to the position of Duke in what is now the city of Kaifeng. It was at this time that he established a new formula for papermaking which consisted of bark, hemp and cotton rag and which subsequently became known as 'Duke Cai's Paper'. This formula was adopted as the standard for papermaking, and remained virtually unchanged for many centuries.

Similarly, the earliest printing techniques can also be traced to China. First developed by Taoist monks in the form of both wooden and stone relief seals carved in reverse, the earliest designs were based on celestial constellations and were most likely used as primitive talismans. By c. AD 600 methods for printing decorative patterns on silk were in use, with woodblock techniques for printing on paper following soon after. The earliest surviving example of a woodblock print on paper is known as the *Jin Gang Jing* or *Diamond Sutra*, dating from AD

蔡 伦

Drawing of Cai Lun (d. AD 121), credited with the invention of paper

868. This work, discovered in 1899 amongst other early Buddhist writings in the 1000 Buddha Cave in Dunhuang, Gansu Province, indicates a highly developed woodcarving technique. Printed in the form of a scroll, the *Diamond Sutra* depicts a sermon by Sakyamuni, the Indian originator of Buddhism, in which he extols the importance of tranquillity of the body and mind.

The tremendous impact of the growth in printing technology cannot be over-estimated. The potential it raised for both the diffusion of information and the spread of religion and culture was unparalleled. By as early as the 9th century printing had also become widely recognized for its enormous commercial potential. In the Chinese classic *The History of the Tang Dynasty (Tang Shu)*, it is noted that a palace petition was submitted to the Emperor in 835: he was requested to forbid the sale of privately printed almanacs until after the release of the official government version to avoid the competition that was costing them great losses in sales.

The actual practice of book design developed early and has a long and important history in China. The Ming dynasty (1368–1644) writer Shao Jingbang refers to AD 636 as the year for the earliest printed book (tantalizingly, he neglected to make any reference to its subject). The degree of sophistication achieved in Chinese printing during the 9th century led to a flourishing printing trade by the 10th. The height of early secular printing came in the Song dynasty (AD 960–1279), when new standards were set for the use of quality materials and special emphasis was placed on the creation of designs that evoked a sense of simplicity, honesty and elegance. Clothbound books from this period used very plain and unadorned covers, relying on titles inscribed by famous calligraphers for their aesthetic appeal. Special attention was paid to the coherence and harmony of the brushed characters in an effort to balance the relationship between those that were dense and those that were spare, as well as between their relative sizes. In this manner the best designs of the period recognized the importance of a strong organic relationship between the title, its subject and the calligraphic characters, effectively unifying the whole.

Woodcuts continued to be used to reproduce well-known calligraphic texts originally engraved on stone tablets. Between AD 1101 and AD 1125 the Emperor Hui Zong commissioned the first woodcut catalogue, documenting the bronze collection of the Imperial Palace. It included a pictorial inventory but also instructions for its circulation within the palace, which may constitute one of the first examples of woodcut printing being used for the purposes of art education.

During the Southern Song dynasty (1127–1279) Emperor Ning Zong sponsored a series of woodcut texts describing a variety of labours and commercial activities. The most famous of these, *Pictures of Tilling and Weaving*, was illustrated by the artists Liu Song-nian and Lou Shou; it portrayed the growing of rice and the production of silk and linen. The texts are highly regarded; with accuracy and detail, they move beyond the portrayals of the elite or scholarly classes and instead document the labours of the peasantry.

Under the Yuan dynasty (1279–1368), woodblock began to take on a new sensitivity as technical development continued to increase. A growing interest in the theatre also provided new subject matter for woodcut artists. The first polychrome prints were introduced towards the end of the Yuan dynasty using a method whereby several colours were simultaneously printed from the same block. During the Ming dynasty (1368–1644) multiple block printing was developed and offered the possibility of more subtle and variable tones.

With a realization of the commercial potential of printing came diversification of materials and methods that continued to yield new possibilities. Etched bronze plates were introduced during the Song dynasty for their ability to stand up to the commercial demands of printing in quantity. It was by this method that the first advertising handbills and paper wrappers were produced for a needle shop in what is now Shandong Province. Shops had already been advertised with coloured flags and hanging signs, but this printed paper for 'Jinan Liu's Fine Needle Shop' represents one of the first forays into printed advertising and commercial design. Illustrated with a highly developed trademark of a white rabbit holding a sewing needle, the inscription reads: 'Note the white rabbit at the front door as a mark.' At the bottom is a further message: 'Purchase fine steel bars and make excellent needles.'

Certainly the most complex of early printed texts was the *Complete Collection of Buddhist Scriptures (Da Zang Jing)*, begun in 971 by Zhang Tu-xin. Requiring twelve years to complete, the entire work comprised 5,048 individual volumes printed from 130,000 individually carved woodblocks. The scale of this project clearly illustrates the difficulty of reproducing texts of great length by the woodblock technique. However, by the 11th century the development of movable typography presented an alternative to the cumbersome block-printing methods.

The actual invention of movable type is credited to Bi Sheng between the years 1041 and 1048. Using carved clay characters which were kiln-fired to increase their strength, Bi Sheng developed a method whereby he could affix the clay blocks to a metal plate coated with wax to hold the pieces securely in place. At the end of a print run the wax could be softened, the characters disassembled and another text composed. Other methods using characters of wood and bronze soon followed, each with its own particular advantages and

A Qing dynasty edition of Pictures of Tilling and Weaving, *originally illustrated by Liu Song-nian and Lou Shou during the Southern Song dynasty (1127–1279).*

Commercial advertising began early. Handbill for Jinan Liu's Fine Needle Shop, Shandong Province, Song dynasty.

Above left: *Wheel pan for the sorting and storage of Chinese characters to be used in the printing of handset texts.*

Above centre and right: *The change from hand-brushed calligraphy to standardized characters was not easily accepted by writers and artists. Two characters in 'Old Song' style, however, show the influence of an ink rubbing of early calligraphy by Yan Zhen-qing that was later engraved in stone* (centre). *Characters in the 'After Song' style* (right) *developed a strong similarity to the calligraphy of Ouyang Xun,* AD 637.

disadvantages. Although these processes were employed in China some four hundred years before Gutenberg's printed bible of 1455, they did not always present a satisfactory solution for the printing of the Chinese language. There were an estimated 47,000 extant characters, of which perhaps 3,000 might be required for a given text, so that the production of multiple copies of characters entailed a sizable outlay of time and a sophisticated storage and retrieval system. In addition, scholars often found the aesthetic quality of the movable type inferior to the unique and distinctive potential of calligraphy on the carved block. For this reason woodblock remained the principal method of printing in China until the advent of modern typographic methods introduced by missionary presses in the 19th century.

In 1814 a British press and the equipment for casting modern Chinese type was installed in Macao after requests from Robert Morrison, the first Protestant missionary in China. Prohibited by the Qing court from printing and distributing his religious tracts, Morrison turned instead to the production of a Chinese dictionary before his operation encountered financial trouble and failed. However, with the conclusion of the Opium War of 1840–42, highly unfair treaties effectively placed large portions of Chinese territory in foreign hands, allowing mission presses to establish themselves in China without fear of censorship.

These treaty concessions sadly underscored the ineptitude of the Qing court and the general weakness of the nation. Growing disillusionment among Chinese intellectuals and students reached a critical point as they banded together in protest to express their dissatisfaction with the hopelessly backward educational system that left the people unprepared for the modern world and vulnerable to foreign aggression. Until this time a long-standing respect for tradition and a concern for continuity had prevented any significant departures from the classical education. Only in 1895, when the scholar-official Kang You-wei presented the Qing court with a long series of proposals known as the 'Ten Thousand Word Memorial', did the educational system undergo any official reconsideration. For this reason, art education was also slow to develop and most individual experimentation went unrecognized. It should be remembered that in China success in the arts rarely depended on artistic ingenuity. Rather, artists were expected to spend the first half of their lives copying the works of a master. In theory, a student could paint a composition that was identical to his master's but by imbuing it with a greater sense of qi – 'spirit' – surpass the quality of the original.

Riding on the momentum of a burgeoning reform movement, artists began to press for changes in the teaching of the arts. Exposure to Western academic methods in studio art originally grew out of demands for courses in scientific and technical drawing. With these curricular changes, reformers hoped to make Chinese education more competitive with that in the West and thus strengthen the nation as a whole. Paradoxically, it was through the foreign settlements along the eastern coastal areas, most notably Shanghai, that examples of Western art and design first found their way into China. Through numerous

Street banners, Foochow Road, Shanghai, 1930s.

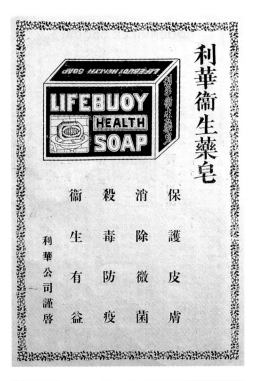

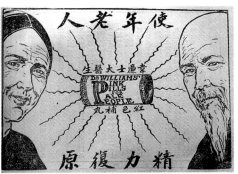

Above, clockwise: *Advertisements for Dr Williams' Pink Pills (The Ladies' Journal, May 1918. Publisher: Shanghai Commercial Press); Lifebuoy Health Soap (Li Hua Co., 1930s); My Dear Cigarettes (Designer: Zhang Di-han for Hua Chen Cigarette Co., 1930s).*

imported periodicals and advertisements Chinese artists were able to see first hand the artworks gracing the European salons of the late 19th century.

The first formalized art and design curriculum in China based on Western methodology was introduced by Liu Hai-su, a native of Jiangsu Province. In 1912, at the age of sixteen, Liu founded the Shanghai Institute of Fine Art. This offered a radical departure from the limited Chinese academic training, which had previously relied on traditional ink and watercolour painting, aerial perspective and linear design. Liu's Western approach revolutionized Chinese art education by introducing the fundamentals of Western oil painting, two-point perspective and the development of source lighting and shadows in still-life compositions. As the first art academy to accept both male and female students and the first to employ the use of nude models, the Shanghai Institute of Fine Art was viewed as a progressive example for combined training in both Chinese and Western traditions.

By the end of the second decade of the 20th century many advertising agencies had been established in China's major cities to act as media agents for foreign companies wishing to expand their foreign trade. This increased demand for artists trained in the Western style further encouraged the development of educational programmes in Western design and advertising. Many

Chinese artists sought fine-arts training in the United States and returned to take up positions in both foreign and domestically run agencies.

The earliest advertising clients in China were foreign manufacturers of soaps, cigarettes and patent medicines. Many companies who relied heavily on advertising and promotion set up their own design departments. The British and American Tobacco Company (BAT), founded in 1902, established an early creative studio in Shanghai which employed numerous Western-trained artists to turn out a constant flow of promotional materials. Advertising departments also developed in conjunction with printing houses, often retaining a degree of autonomy to provide design and marketing services for a broader range of commercial activities. One of the earliest such services was located at Shanghai's Oriental Press, established under French guidance with Ke Lian-hui serving as the chief designer. In the 1920s, Ke – with the help of his sons Ke Dao-zhong, Ke Ting and Ke Luo – formed his own company, called the Lianhui Art Association. Together they edited the typographic guide *Models for the English Alphabet*, which was the first to address the graphic needs of a foreign clientele.

While the full effect of this relatively sudden introduction of Western ideas, products and lifestyles on Chinese society is hard to gauge, the designs from the period are certainly indicative of its range of influence. As an immediate challenge to centuries of continuity and insularity, Western design practices brought a host of changes, with clearly mixed results. What becomes increasingly evident in the chapters to follow, however, is the overwhelming ability of Chinese culture to absorb distinctly foreign ideas while retaining its own identity. Tremendous influences from the West are undeniably evident, yet the designs that seem to have survived the creative test of time are those that have found a distinctive Chinese voice. They are successful not only in the immediate sense of fulfilling the important task of communication, but in their evolution beyond the didactic and superficially ornamental. By carefully and creatively expanding on China's inherent design traditions the works reproduced in this book offer a convincing testament to the beauty, continuity and endurance of Chinese culture as a whole.

Advertisement for Koo Pun Beauty Soap, 1935–36.

2 · May Fourth and the Formative Years

There is no pattern for straw shoes,
They shape up as one weaves them.

Old Hunanese Proverb

During the early years of the 20th century, following the collapse of the Qing dynasty, the political and cultural future of China was extremely uncertain. In an atmosphere of domestic discontent and growing Western influence, artists eagerly engaged in a wide range of artistic experimentation as they tried to reinvigorate the nation's cultural climate. Art schools that had previously taught solely in the traditional Chinese manner began to broaden their curricula to accommodate the influential ideas of the Western academic styles. While a functional knowledge of modern design had existed in China since the early 1900s, it had remained virtually unrecognized as a legitimate profession, with work in advertising, publication design and packaging most frequently relegated to classically trained painters and illustrators. As a consequence of the academic and cultural reforms sweeping the nation, many young artists involved in the expanding commercial trade struggled to free the concept of graphic design from the many conventions that had limited a full realization of its unique communicative and expressive potential.

Widespread support for these new explorations was readily found in the artistic and literary circles formed in the aftermath of the May Fourth student demonstrations of 1919. Originally organized to protest at the government's acceptance of the unfavourable Versailles peace treaty after the First World War, the demonstrations represented at their deepest level a demand for major social and political reform, a rejection of China's feudal heritage and a call for comprehensive modernization. As a national uprising and subsequently as a movement, May Fourth was unprecedented in drawing broad popular support from workers, students and intellectuals alike. While its commitment to

Above: *The May Fourth demonstrators, Shanghai, 1919.*

Opposite: The Dividing Line in Love, *1929. Designer: Qian Jun-tao. Publisher: The Oriental Book Company.*

Lu Xun and his study in Shaoxing.

change aroused considerable suspicion in a country that held dear to traditional values, the movement set important precedents for progressive thought that would last well through the century.

The educational and cultural implications of the May Fourth Movement focused special interest on the arts during the Twenties. Reformers engaged in lengthy and often emotional debates over the role of modern art and design in the renewal of Chinese society. The most sensitive discussions centred on the extent to which Western influence was desirable in a country torn between respect for continuity and tradition and an intense desire for modernization.

Since the turn of the century, examples of Western art and design had begun to appear in China through the importation of illustrated books and journals for its foreign population. Because of the distance these materials travelled and the time it took for them to be absorbed into the domestic environment, the earliest influences to appear in Chinese designs did so considerably after their popularity at home had faded. Throughout the Twenties traces of the organic and curvilinear characteristics of the late Art Nouveau period could be recognized on the covers of popular Chinese books and magazines, making the re-cycling of what had originally begun in the West as an Asian-influenced design movement ironically complete. Although somewhat modified to accommodate a growing interest in geometric form, the Chinese applications of the Art Nouveau style succeeded in imparting their highly characteristic penchant for human solitude, pensiveness and self-reflection. With their stylized veneer of Asian exoticism, images of the late Art Nouveau period needed little adaptation to become immediately appealing to the Chinese public. An essential cause of this popular acceptance was its strong visual reaffirmation of the human spirit. For the Chinese, who were just beginning to confront the onslaught of conflicting ideological and moral standards of Western culture, the romanticized images of contemplation embodied in the Art Nouveau style seemed both sympathetic and reassuring.

At the same time, a small but vocal group of designers declared that this direct importation of foreign images was dangerous and would lead to the deterioration of China's national aesthetic identity. Influenced by the ideas of the writer and scholar Lu Xun, a loose association of designers led by Tao Yuanqing began to explore alternative design directions through the study of traditional Chinese patterns and decorative motifs. It was their belief that design should grow out of personal experience, using the aesthetic language inherent in their own culture. Only in this way could graphic design succeed in communicating with a broad cross-section of the Chinese people and reflect an appropriate sense of its unique artistic origins. Such an assessment paralleled Lu Xun's own studied interest in the implementation of the common vernacular language. Long relegated to the lower classes, this form of popular speech was elevated by Lu Xun to a prominent place in the national literature. The change thereby brought to the general public's access to new writing and eventually to widespread education was monumental. Although Western missionaries had employed limited use of vernacular language for several decades in order to reach the greatest number of potential converts, it was only through Lu Xun's efforts during the Twenties and Thirties that the use of such language became commonplace. Lu Xun's documentation of the lives and struggles of society's outcasts was significant not only for its implicit ability to explore the darker side of life with new vividness and clarity, but also for the strong support it fuelled for similar tendencies in the visual arts.

This new interest in the rendering of human destiny in both literature and design can be seen as a natural outgrowth of a rapidly changing world. The sudden influx of new scientific discoveries and advances in theoretical knowledge as a result of the educational reforms of the May Fourth Movement had seemed all the more dramatic in China because of its highly isolated past. The introduction into China of Einstein's theory of relativity and Freud's study of the unconscious left profound effects on academic and intellectual circles and shook their confidence in the physical world. These themes were quickly

Tao Yuan-qing in his bedroom, Hangzhou, 1928.

Above: The Short Story Magazine, *August 1927. Designer: Chen Zhi-fo. Publisher: Shanghai Commercial Press. 26.5 x 19.0 cm.*

Right: The Ladies' Journal, *October 1931. Designer: Zhang Ling-tao. Publisher: Shanghai Commercial Press. 26.5 x 19.0 cm.*

Opposite:

Above: Blood and Love. *Author: Jin Man-chen. Publisher: Shanghai Modern Publications.*

Below: The Wild Grass, *July 1927. Author: Lu Xun. Designer: Sun Fu-xi, with Lu Xun's calligraphy. Publisher: Shanghai Beixin Book Company. 20.0 x 13.7 cm.*

adopted by artists, who saw the aesthetic implications of such discoveries leading to a gradual de-materialization of the physical object, in favour of the exploration of more spiritual impulses. Increasing numbers of references were made to creativity, which emanated from a deeply rooted 'inner necessity' and which placed a higher value on subjective experience and emotional manifestations of the soul.

Such preoccupations marked a major departure from classic pictorial themes and brought with them a significant re-evaluation of the traditional concepts of formal composition and structure. By striving to give new expression to highly complex and emotional concepts, a radical break was also made in the independent exploration of line, form and colour. Traditionally, artists sought to unify these elements in an attempt to capture nature's elusive spirit. To them the unification of such physical components was important because they succeeded in giving harmony and balance to highly conventional subjects and were thus seen as inseparable from the creation of a descriptive image. With the move away from classical representation, artists and designers were now free to explore the uninhibited use of these elements as they pleased. As a consequence, line, form and colour began to be explored more for their singular emotional and functional values, allowing artists to embark on a long course of creative abstraction that distinctly modified the long-standing objectives of Chinese painting and design.

While the May Fourth Movement was enormously important in introducing a new aesthetic vision for Chinese art and design, it was also significant in establishing a strong collaborative relationship between writers and designers. Although China had a tradition of famous artists creating calligraphic titles for poetry, or illustrations to accompany a story, many of the new May Fourth illustrators attempted to expand the notions of visual communication by creating images as independent accompaniment to a written text. Rather than render a scene from a novel as a visual excerpt, artists embarked on a process of experimentation that allowed the visual design to project with equal importance the thematic and emotional contents of the book itself. This conscious rejection of the traditional narrative function of illustration and its tendency for literal depiction signalled yet another move toward artistic abstraction and opened the way for the free growth of modern design in the years to come.

Lu Xun and the New Literature and Design

Perhaps more than any other individual it was the writer and scholar Lu Xun who truly legitimized modern Chinese design by encouraging a full exploration of its expressive potential. Until this time, books rarely featured more than simple handpainted calligraphic titles on their covers. Colour was kept to a minimum and any graphic patterning or decoration that did appear bore no relationship to the book's contents. Through Lu Xun's tireless efforts to revitalize Chinese literature came a growing recognition of the enormous potential for both writing and design that would touch the interests and experiences of a growing middle class. By tradition, Chinese literature had been viewed as the property of a classically trained elite, inaccessible and generally without application to the lives of the great majority of Chinese people. Lu Xun and the participants of the New Literature and Design Movement sought to change this exclusivity by reconsidering the aesthetic character of their works and by paying special attention to the needs of their new audience.

As a great admirer of Western printmaking, Lu Xun also introduced the techniques of modern woodblock through a series of illustrated books and practical workshops. His favourite works were those of the German Expressionists, particularly Käthe Kollwitz, whose emotional renderings of human struggle paralleled his own determination to record the inequities of

modern life. Letters between Lu Xun and his colleagues fully underscored his belief in the social responsibility of art and design, a subject never before raised in professional circles. As Lu Xun proclaimed: 'Art represents the thoughts of a period and the ideas of the nation. In other words, it is the outlook of a nation's spirit. If the spirit changes direction then art will follow the change as well.' It was this vision of art as a barometer of the national consciousness that won Lu Xun the admiration of younger writers and designers of the May Fourth Movement, who were engaged in a national struggle to liberate their professions from centuries of conformity.

While he readily encouraged young designers to learn from Western techniques, Lu Xun also insisted that the random application of imported taste was meaningless, and even detrimental, if designers were ignorant of their own unique design heritage. By encouraging designers to study the use of traditional pattern, as found in China's early clay pottery and bronze vessels, as well as figurative imagery from bas-relief stone carvings, Lu tapped a frequently overlooked source of indigenous inspiration. The incorporation of such themes in Lu Xun's own works and those of his followers showed a renewed sensitivity to their culture and led to the development of a strong national artistic identity that remains fundamental to Chinese design to this day.

Above right: Sprout, *January 1930. Editor: Lu Xun. Publisher: Guanghua Book Company. 20.6 x 15.2 cm.*

Right: Literature and Art Study Quarterly, *February 1930. Publisher: Shanghai Dajiang Book Store. 21.0 x 14.8 cm.*

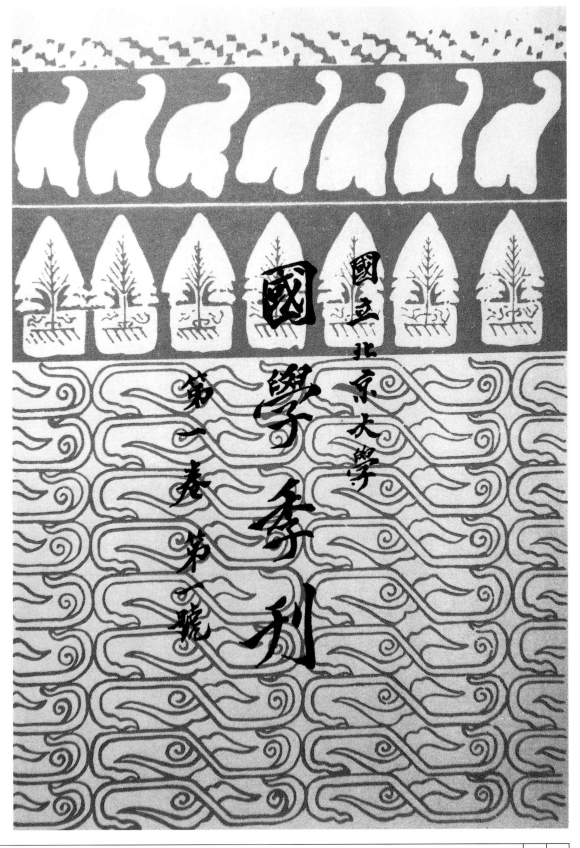

National Learning and Culture, *January 1923.*
Calligraphy by Cai Yuan-pei.
Publisher: Beijing University Press.
25.7 x 18.5 cm.

The Indigenous Imagery of Tao Yuan-qing

Tao Yuan-qing was without doubt one of the most influential Chinese graphic designers of the 20th century. Inspired and encouraged by Lu Xun, Tao succeeded in developing an approach to book design that was significant for its rediscovery and implementation of traditional Chinese patterns and motifs. Ranging from prehistoric carvings to Tang dynasty sculpture (AD 618–906) as his sources, Tao Yuan-qing studied the historical representations of the human body as inspiration for his own figurative renderings. Often composed of flat shapes in profile view, his designs suggest the long tradition of stone transfers or 'rubbings' used as a means to document China's ancient carved tablets. His compositions, using light and expressive brushstrokes, are also indicative of his training in both traditional Chinese painting and Western watercolour techniques, which he merges to form lyrical and highly expressive visual statements.

Left: Wandering, *August 1929. Author: Lu Xun. Designer: Tao Yuan-qing. Publisher: Beijing Beixin Book Company. 19.3 x 13.7 cm.*

Opposite, top to bottom: Dawn Blossoms Plucked at Dusk, *September 1928. Author: Lu Xun. Designer: Tao Yuan-qing. Publisher: Beijing Weiming Association. 20.2 x 14.5 cm.*

Worker Zweilov, *June 1927. Translator: Lu Xun. Designer: Tao Yuan-qing. Publisher: Beijing Beixin Book Company. 20.2 x 14.2 cm.*

Fuxi and Nüwa. *Rubbing from Late Han dynasty stone engraving. Xinjin, Sichuan Province.*

Far right: Hometown, *May 1926. Author: Xu Jin-wen. Designer: Tao Yuan-qing. Publisher: Beijing Beixin Book Company. 19.3 x 13.4 cm.*

夫略綏惠人工

阿爾志跋綏夫 著　魯迅 譯

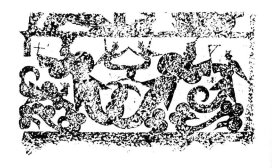

The Indigenous Imagery of Tao Yuan-qing

In his search to unify graphic imagery and literary content, Tao Yuan-qing was also responsible for a new creative philosophy that stressed strong collaboration between artist and writer. His cover design for *Depressed Symbol* (1924) marked the beginning of his own long and invaluable association with Lu Xun, who claimed that Tao's works were free from the clichés of the period and representative of 'China's eternal soul'. Among the many covers he produced, his design for *Wandering* (1926, p. 29) was often cited as his best work. As Lu Xun explained, Tao's compositions brought to light 'fresh colours' which 'converge with an

Depressed Symbol, *December 1924. Translator: Lu Xun. Designer: Tao Yuan-qing. Publisher: Beijing Weiming Association. 20.0 x 13.8 cm.*

Below: *Detail from Selected Tang and Song Stories, 1927. Editor: Lu Xun. Designer: Tao Yuan-qing. Publisher: Shanghai Beixin Book Company. 19.4 x 13.8 cm.*

international current of thought and at the same time maintain China's national character'. Such goals were often lost amongst other young and impressionable designers of the time, who lacked the same selective and discerning vision that gave balance to the works of Tao Yuan-qing and the best of the May Fourth artists. It was Tao's belief that only by continually referring to and integrating China's traditional visual motifs could a design maintain strong emotional connections to traditional culture and project an authentic Chinese spirit.

Right: A Jar of Wine, 1930. Author: Xu Jin-wen. Designer: Tao Yuan-qing. Publisher: Shanghai Beixin Book Company. 20.0 x 14.0 cm.

Far Right: Out of the Ivory Tower, December 1925. Translator: Lu Xun. Designer: Tao Yuan-qing. Publisher: Beijing Weiming Association. 20.4 x 14.4 cm.

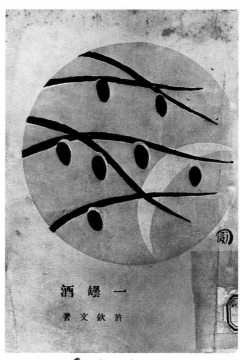

一鑻酒

著文欽許

出了象牙之塔

日本 廚川白村 著

Contribution Magazine

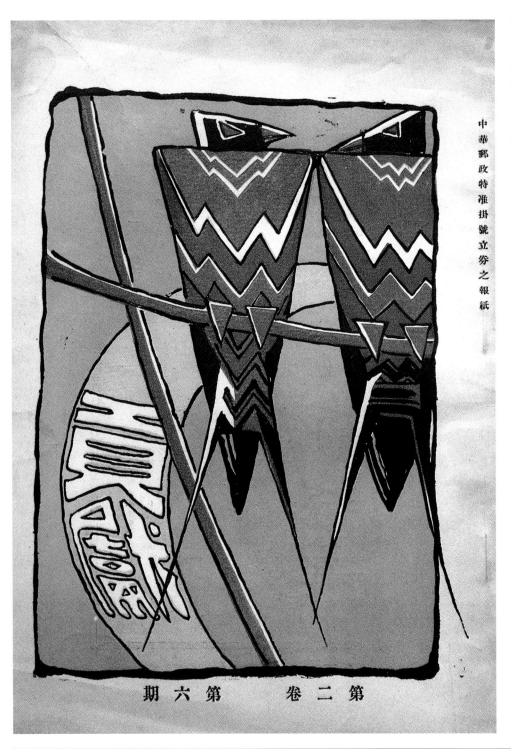

中華郵政特准掛號立劵之報紙

期 六 第　　卷 二 第

Founded after a massive popular uprising known as the 1925–27 Revolution, *Contribution* stated its intention of creating a balanced forum for the circulation of diverse but informed points of view. Its bi-monthly collection of articles included selections of literature, art, education, culture and politics, with the only criterion being that the magazine establish a balance between respected traditional thinking and reformist trends. In this manner the editors believed that *Contribution* could be an important link in the circulation and mixing of prominent ideas and aesthetics during this critical point in China's political and cultural development.

Respected for its consistently creative cover designs by established designers, *Contribution* intended its changing visual styles to reflect the same eclectic character as its contents. Suggestions of the growing popularity of early Art Deco, mixed with a flowing Asian organicism, make *Contribution* an important pioneer of modern Chinese design in both theory and in practice. Its lack of interest in establishing a standardized logotype also highlighted the editors' intrinsic belief in upholding the artistic integrity of its designers, who often achieved a sophisticated integration of the *Contribution* name within the body of the design.

Contribution, *April 1928. Designer: Liu Ji-piao. Publisher: Shanghai Yingying Book House. 26.0 x 19.0 cm.*

Top: Contribution, *August 1928. Publisher: Shanghai Yingying Book House. 26.0 x 19.0 cm.*

Above: Contribution, *October 1928. Designer: Wu Da-yu. Publisher: Shanghai Yingying Book House. 26.0 x 19.0 cm.*

Right: Contribution, *March 1928. Designer: Fang Yun. Publisher: Shanghai Yingying Book House. 26.0 x 19.0 cm.*

大黑狼的故事

3 · The Shanghai Style

Shanghai, city of amazing paradoxes and fantastic contrasts . . . native emporiums with lacquered ducks and salt eggs . . . bursts of advertising color . . . musicians compensating with gusto for lack of harmony and rhythm . . . modern motors throbbing with the power of eighty horses march abreast with tattered one-man power rickshaws . . . Shanghai the bizarre.

All About Shanghai, 1934

During the Twenties and Thirties Shanghai achieved a worldwide reputation as Asia's preeminent metropolis. It was a city of vitality and vice in which East and West collided in an atmosphere of forced coexistence. As many as twenty-three distinct foreign nationalities mingled within the boundaries of the international settlement. Entire cultures, with all their regional habits and peculiarities, were transplanted from Europe and America for the benefit of the individuals who found themselves involved in the politics or commerce of the region. The major concession zones in Shanghai proper represented eight foreign powers, each implanting its own customs, food and architecture on Chinese soil.

With the abolition of the official examination system in 1905, which for decades had determined who would succeed and who would fail in their desire for some degree of wealth, fame or influence, cities like Shanghai offered new possibilities for occupational self-determination and advancement. As Shanghai was the first Chinese city to undergo modern urbanization, it became a natural focus for the activities of a generation of writers and artists who sought the sanctuary of the city for the new lifestyles and creative opportunities it offered. While one of the strongest criticisms of the city was the legal autonomy the foreign concessions maintained, the same powers that put the residents beyond the legal reach of the Chinese courts also had the effect of providing relatively safe cover for the artists, writers and intellectuals who chose to work in more avant-garde styles. With punishment for outspokenness a certainty under the Qing court and the threat of violent reprisal a possibility under the succeeding governments, thousands of Chinese scholars and intel-

Above: A Great Love, c.1930. *Designer: Qian Jun-tao. Publisher: Shanghai Kaiming Book Store.*

Opposite: The Big Black Wolf, 1930. *Designer: Qian Jun-tao. Publisher: Shanghai Kaiming Book Store.*

The University Press, Shanghai, offers its own advertising and public relations services, 1934.

lectuals moved to Shanghai, making it an effective base not only for dissident activity but for professional recognition and success.

As early as 1902 advertising agencies working through the media of outdoor signboards and printed advertising began to transform the urban landscape with images of modern life. Literary and artistic journals were also frequent sources for images of predominately Western lifestyles. It has been estimated that between 1910 and 1930 alone Chinese publishing expanded by six-fold. Part of this demand for reading material was due to an increase in the literacy rate, but it was also the result of a growing working class in search of entertainment. The creation of progressive newspapers and magazines that wrote in the vernacular style provided the perfect vehicle for the introduction of a wide range of new ideas and foreign products.

Faced with a growing demand for creative design services, the major printing houses in Shanghai developed full-time advertising and design departments. While their primary function was to provide regular cover proposals and publicity materials for their own books and magazines, these departments often advertised their creative and marketing services to the general public. The University Press of Shanghai was well known for its independent consulting and public relations departments. In an ad from 1934, the Press stated: 'Modern advertising is an exact science. When you are ill you see a physician; When you are in trouble you see a lawyer; When your business needs new life, see an advertising expert.'

The great majority of advertising revenue through the Twenties came from pharmaceutical, cosmetic and tobacco companies. Capitalizing on popular interest in the lifestyles and social values of the West, these industries hoped to position their products in a new and progressive context. Paying particular attention to the changing roles of women in Chinese society, cigarette and cosmetic companies eagerly sought to re-define their image through heavy advertising. As in the West, smoking and the use of make-up became symbols of a newly attained independence and freedom for the modern woman.

As a natural response to the influx of Western culture, Chinese designers frequently drew inspiration from readily available European and American publications. Perhaps the visual style most frequently adapted in this period was derived from the Art Deco movement, which was enjoying simultaneous popularity in Europe and America. Originating in Paris with the 1925 Exposition Internationale des Arts Décoratifs, the Art Deco style became known for its experimentation with geometric ornamentation, bold colours and strong patterns. With great ease and vitality, the stylishness of Art Deco was transplanted to the cosmopolitan milieu of Shanghai. Normally considered a movement

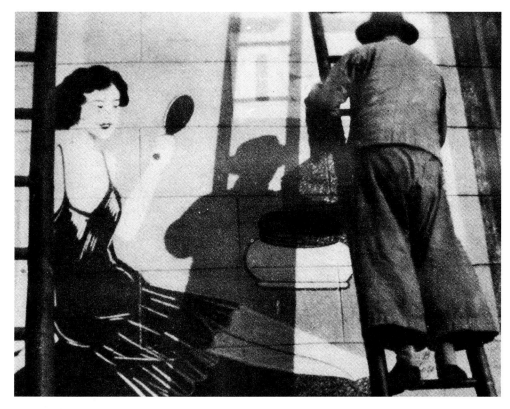

Left: *Painting billboards for cosmetics advertising, c.1930.*

Below, far left: *Advertisement for Butterfly Perfume, c.1937. Designer: Gao Kui-zhang.*

Below left: *Advertisement for toothpaste, c.1937.*

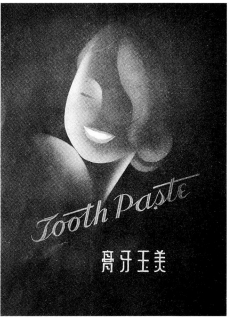

Above: *The Lang Liang-xin Shop (Gallery of Kind Heart), photographed in the 1930s, was an example of the traditional architecture that inspired much of Chen Zhi-fo's complex graphic design.*

Right: Modern Student, *June 1931. Editor: Liu Da-jie. Designer: Chen Zhi-fo. Publisher: Shanghai Dadong Book Company.*

Far right: *Advertisement for* Art and Life Magazine, *1937. Designer: Zhang De-rong.*

devoted to exuberant displays of wealth and fashion, Art Deco found its place in the artistic traditions of China more as an outgrowth of an already existing geometric architectural tradition. Coming to a culture with such a strong decorative heritage, the geometric and patterned compositions of Art Deco only succeeded in fuelling further the renewed interests in China's own past. For this reason Chinese Art Deco achieved a masterful synthesis of colour, shape and pattern that transcended many superficial Western applications.

The adoption of Synthetic Cubism into the general vocabulary of European Art Deco also had its parallels in Chinese artistic traditions. With the introduction of the multiple viewpoint and subsequent loss of three-dimensional perspective, the European Cubists effectively established design as a vital element in their creative process. Similarly, classical Chinese painting disregarded Western perspective as developed by Leonardo in favour of planimetric space. This technique allowed the artist to extend the field of the picture plane without visual distortion and lent itself appropriately to modern design. As a result, images of the human body in the Chinese Art Deco style are frequently seen as renderings reduced to simple linear or geometric divisions of form. Many of these images also contradict any sense of anatomical correctness, yet successfully communicate the essence of the subject matter with great simplicity and speed.

During the Twenties great advances were also made in the development and stylization of typographic forms. Chinese characters have historically lent themselves to creative distortion and manipulation as a means of communicating further the concept of a phrase or sentence. Because of the individual nature of each graphic work, typefaces were rarely standardized, instead reflecting the nuances and subtleties of the particular composition. In this way designers could introduce their own variations to achieve a higher degree of compatibility with the visual image. Thus we see in the work of the period an amazing typographic range, often incorporating abstract symbols or designs as a part of the character itself, and thereby extending its conceptual meaning. To this day, major titles for books and magazines in China are rendered by hand, with cast type more often being used for body copy and advertising headlines.

Early in the Twenties artist associations were formed to discuss the topics of the day and to view and exhibit their members' work. Since graphic design was an occupation almost solely limited to and defined by the commerce of the city, the designers within Shanghai kept closely abreast of one another's activities. Meetings were frequently held in tea houses, wine shops and restaurants, for this afforded the members an excuse for getting out of their homes and studios and sampling what was new. When particular styles came into vogue, all of Shanghai seemed to produce designs with elements in common. Thus the Shanghai Style, with its roots in European Art Deco, found strong support amongst designers in the Twenties and Thirties. Once this style was confirmed as the symbol of contemporary sophistication and modernism, it became implanted in the design vocabulary until it was either exhausted or replaced.

Book cover, 1936. Designer: Zheng Ren-ze.

The Graphic Lyricism of Qian Jun-tao

Far left: Another Wife, c. 1930. Designer: Qian Jun-tao.

Left: Killing Beauty, 1931. Designer: Qian Jun-tao. Publisher: Shanghai Shuimo Book Store.

Of the many designers of the early avant-garde, Qian Jun-tao was especially instrumental in relating visual design to broader concepts of the creative experience. Having undertaken early studies in music, Qian sought to apply his knowledge of music theory to his book-cover compositions of the Twenties. Of particular interest to him was the visual embodiment of both melody and rhythm, characteristics that have remained evident in his work throughout his long career.

Born in 1906 in Zhejiang Province, Qian Jun-tao began to compose and publish lyrical songs in the magazine *New Women* during the early Twenties. It was during this same period that he also began a long and cherished friendship with Lu Xun and the influential artists Chen Zhi-fo and Situ Qiao. From the creation of his first designs, under the guidance of Tao Yuan-qing, Qian developed an early interest in graphic pattern and repetitive motifs. His ongoing research into organic Japanese design brought with it the ultimate recognition of its Chinese origins. Thus he began a study of the ancient art of Dunghuan, as well as ancient stone carvings and bronze designs from the Zhou and Qin dynasties (1027–206 BC).

In his book-cover designs from the Twenties, Qian Jun-tao exhibited a free-spirited graphic simplicity that, while illustrating, avoided literalness. Through the use of harmonious patterns and stylized organic forms, his work hints of the popular Art Deco style but succeeds in maintaining a strong Chinese identity. As Qian once explained: 'One cannot tell which country a work is from if it is modern but without its own national character. On the other hand, if a work cannot go beyond its own traditional form, then the work has no future either. Maintaining the national character does not mean just imitating or borrowing. Such design alone would have no artistic meaning or value.

By the early Thirties Qian Jun-tao had become a major figure in the Progressive Movement, anticipating the growing interest in geometry and the new rational order. Yet, unlike many designs of the period, his typographic forms and tightly structured compositions can be seen as a natural evolution of a highly personal design style.

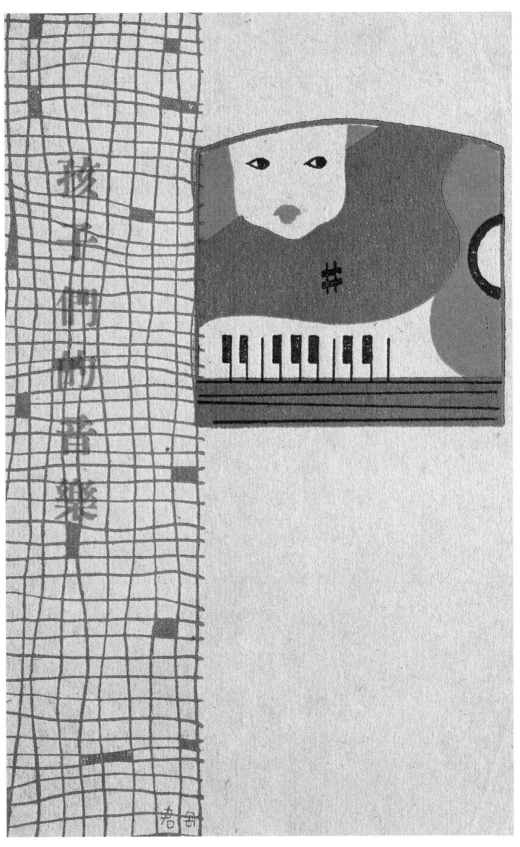

Top: *Book cover illustration, c. 1930.*
Designer: Qian Jun-tao.

Above: The Short Story Magazine,
February 1929. Designer: Qian Jun-tao.
Publisher: Shanghai Commercial Press.
26.3 x 18.0 cm.

Right: Children's Music, *c. 1930.*
Designer: Qian Jun-tao. Publisher: Shanghai
Kaiming Book Store.

Chen Zhi-fo: The Primacy of Pattern

For the artist Chen Zhi-fo (1898–1962), pattern was an intrinsic part of daily life. From his early explorations in the sketching and study of foliage and landscape to his later concern for geometric repetition and architectural structure, Chen was preoccupied with the rhythmical and linear forms around him. As an art student he had specialized in machine-woven pattern design and had been sent to Japan where he learned more about the manufacture of traditional fabric motifs by modern methods. During his years there, Chen spent much of his time in libraries, bookstores and museums, collecting materials that would ultimately influence his own design.

By the mid-Thirties Chen Zhi-fo was engaged in whimsical designs for book and magazine covers which were loosely based on traditional Chinese architecture and handicrafts. Compositions prepared in conjunction with Lu Xun, such as *Experience of Creation* and *Lu Xun's Self-Selected Collection*, displayed Chen's particular interest in the decorative fretwork of traditional temples and step motifs, and also made abstract references to domestic post and lintel construction. In his work for *Modern Student* magazine, human figures emerge from his complex designs, only to disappear again upon the discovery of some other elusive detail. Chen Zhi-fo revelled in such slow discoveries of the eye; his mastery of natural camouflage led to continual surprises and a playfulness in design that denied the hurried glances and inattentive habits of modern life.

Far left: Modern Student, *July 1931. Editor: Liu Da-jie. Designer: Chen Zhi-fo. Publisher: Shangai Dadong Book Company. 21.5 x 15.2 cm.*

Left: Lu Xun's Self-Selected Collection, *March 1933. Author: Lu Xun. Designer: Chen Zhi-fo, with calligraphy by Ju Xun. Publisher: Tianma Book Store. 18.4 x 13.0 cm.*

Right: Experience of Creation, *June 1933. Designer: Chen Zhi-fo, with calligraphy by Lu Xun. Publisher: Tianma Book Store. 18.7 x 13.0 cm.*

The Popular Acceptance of Art Deco

The growth in the Chinese urban middle class during the Twenties brought about an entirely new market for art, literature, entertainment and leisure. Low-grade fiction, composed to a large degree of love stories with classical themes and disparagingly referred to as 'Mandarin Duck and Butterfly' style, quickly came under attack by proponents of the New Literature Movement who sought to improve the quality of popular writing. Shanghai, which had become the centre for progressive lifestyles and a showcase for imported Western tastes, witnessed a tremendous growth in new books and magazines which introduced the latest artistic styles and popular fashions from Europe and America. It was in this manner that many cultural influences of diverse origins found their way into the Chinese design vocabulary.

The roots of the Shanghai Style, in particular, can be traced in part to the imported designs of American and European Art Deco of the Twenties. With a strong predilection for images of fashion, transportation and sport, many young Chinese of the burgeoning middle class were attracted to Art Deco design for its representation of modern life. While the Western forms of Art Deco originally embodied the ideals of a predominantly wealthy and carefree society, the Shanghai Style proved appealing to a more populist audience, who were drawn to it for its novelty and exotic flavour. Using crisp lines, geometric forms and a flattening of pictorial space, the Shanghai Style borrowed freely from the formal techniques of the Cubists. In addition, many patterns and motifs found in traditional Chinese decorative arts were easily incorporated into these designs. In this manner the Shanghai Style succeeded not only in suggesting an international influence, but was also able to maintain a decidedly Chinese flair, making it an effective visual accompaniment to the developing fiction of the New Literature.

Opposite: Erosion, *1930.*
Detail of cover. Author: Mao
Dun. Publisher: Shanghai
Kaiming Book Store.

Right: Disconsolation,
1929. Publisher: Shanghai
Modern Publications 18.8 x
13.0 cm.

The Popular Acceptance of Art Deco

Above: Two Women, *1930. Author: Hua Han. Publisher: The Oriental Book Company.* 19.0 x 13.2 cm.

Above right: The Trilogy of Love, *1931. Author: Ceng Jing-ke. Publisher: Shanghai New Times Press.* 19.0 x 13.5 cm.

Right: Two Stars, *1933. Author: Ceng Jing-ke. Publisher: Shanghai New Times Press.* 20.0 x 13.5 cm.

自剖 徐志摩

供口 郭雄子著 中華書局印行

Top left: Self-Analysis, 1928. Author: Xu Zhi-mo. Publisher: Shanghai New Moon Book Store. 19.0 x 13.2 cm.

Bottom left: Fading, 1931. Publisher: Shanghai Taidong Book Company. 18.8 x 13.0 cm.

Top right: The Mouth of the Volcano, 1930. Author: Xu Jie. Publisher: Shanghai Lehua Book Company. 18.4 x 12.7 cm.

Left: Verbal Confession, 1930. Author: Guo Zi-xun. Publisher: Shanghai China Book Company. 18.5 x 13.0 cm.

Masters of Advertising

Throughout the Twenties and Thirties Shanghai designers produced magnificent posters and printed advertisements in their unique version of the Art Deco style. The new acceptance and use of cosmetics during this period brought a sudden influx of competitive advertising, as manufacturers stood to make enormous profits from a new class of professional working women. Similarly, the recent introduction of 'ready-to-wear' clothing also benefited from advertisements in the Art Deco style, which gave the concept credibility and suggested its foreign influence.

Several designers, Zhang Qing-hong among them, were particularly skilled in black-and-white advertising methods, creating images of simplicity and clarity for their client's products and services. Their dynamic compositions, knowledgeable use of tonal effects and strong typographic treatments gave the designs a visual elegance and assured maximum public attention.

The reputation of Shanghai as Asia's capital for vice also inspired numerous public-service posters. Full of emotional force and skilful in concept, such compositions achieved the same degree of sophistication as commercial advertising.

Opposite, top, left to right:
Watches and clocks poster, 1936. Designer: Zhao Zi-xiang.

Loans for agricultural construction advertisement, c. 1937. Designer: Chen Qing-ru.

Cigars advertisement, c. 1937. Designer: Zhao Zi-xiang.

Opposite, bottom, left to right:
Cosmetics poster, 1936. Designer: Wang Yi-chang.

Watches and clocks advertisement, c. 1937. Designer: Zhang Qing-hong.

Stockings poster, 1936. Designer: Chen Shi-jun.

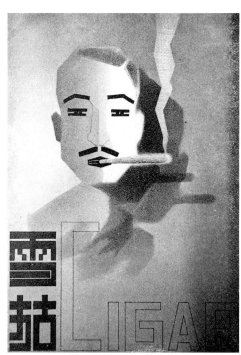

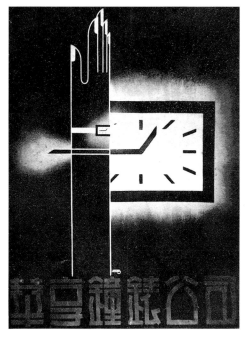

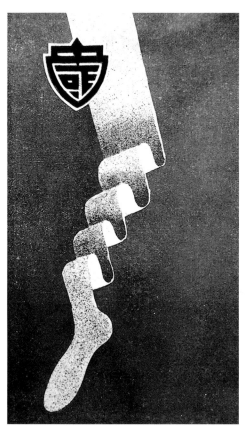

Opposite, above left: *Silk umbrellas poster, 1936. Designer: Zhao Zi-xiang.*

Opposite, below left: *South East Detective Agency poster, 1936. Designer: Chi Ning.*

Left: *Fashion show poster, 1936. Designer: Chi Ning.*

Above: *Newsprint Papers poster, 1936. Designer: Xu Xiao-xia.*

Right: *Fish market poster, 1936. Designer: Xu Min-zhi.*

The Ark 1934–35

Established in 1934, *The Ark* began as a magazine devoted to general aspects of living and family life. With its title intended only as a conceptual reference to the Biblical event, *The Ark* had no real religious pretensions. Rather, it sought to promote itself as a broad informational journal intent on recognizing the endangered future of human relationships and family bonds. Its vividly illustrated covers seem oddly futuristic and cerebral, making it an unusual monthly magazine for its time. While its cover designers remained largely uncredited, great care in its art direction succeeded in maintaining a consistently high degree of artistic ingenuity. Three-dimensional renderings of its logo in rotational orbit of a symbolic earth were a frequent illustrational device, and its varying designs implied the breadth of information contained within.

Although many covers from this period suggest the strong influence of Art Deco, *The Ark* was also careful to display a distinct Chinese sensibility. Freeflowing organic tendrils and subtle references to Asian flora continually reappear, reinforcing a sense of Chinese identity and striking an interesting aesthetic balance between Eastern tradtion and the influential graphic modernism of the West.

Above left: The Ark, *April 1935. Publisher: The Ark Press, Mid-China Printing Company, Tianjin.*

Above right: The Ark, *November 1935. Designer: Liu Xiao-mo. Publisher: The Ark Press, Mid-China Printing Company, Tianjin.*

Above: The Ark, *December 1935. Publisher: The Ark Press, Mid-China Printing Company, Tianjin.*

Right: The Ark, *August 1935. Publisher: The Ark Press, Mid-China Printing Company, Tianjin.*

文學

第一卷第四號

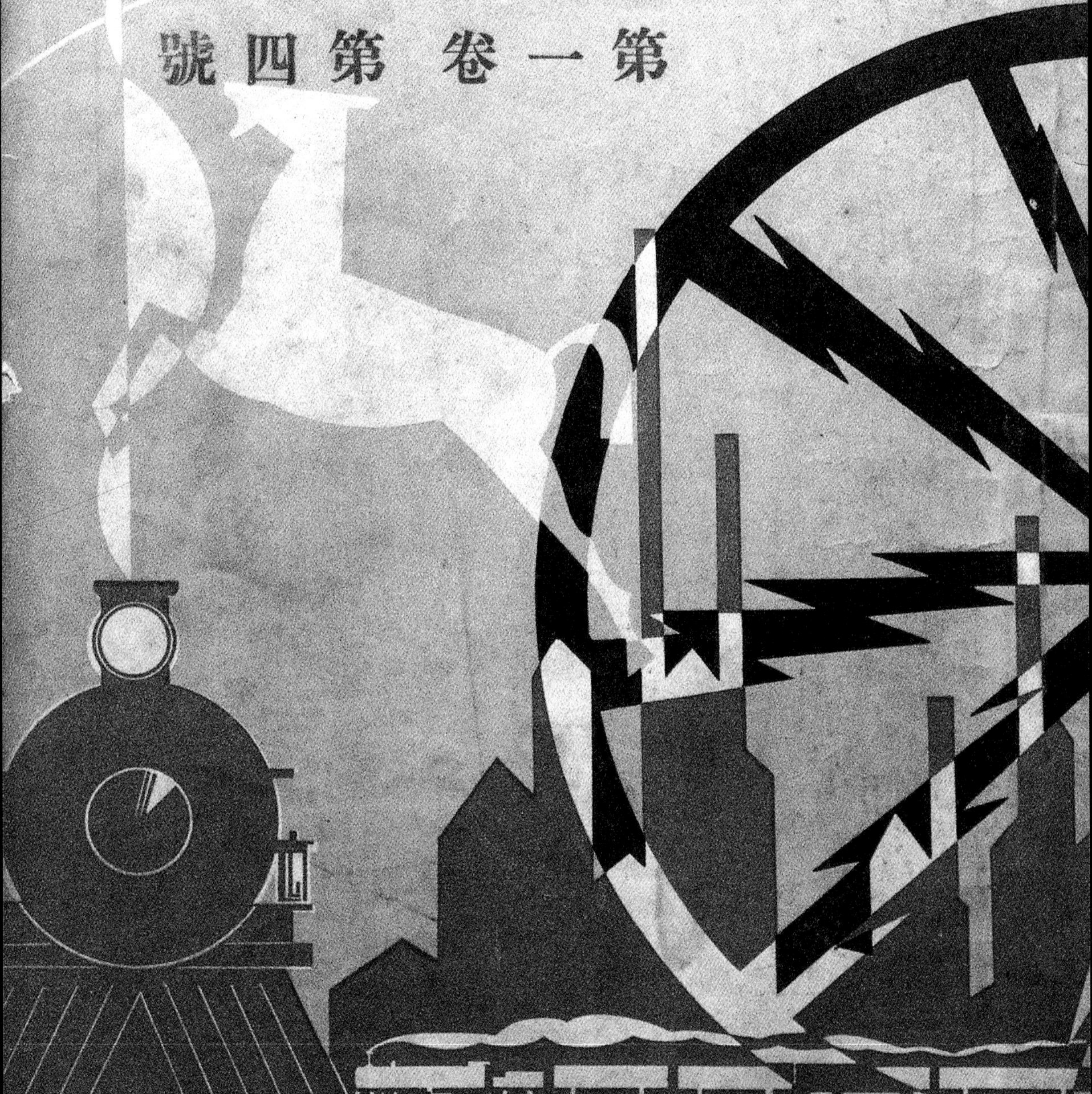

文學社編輯　　生活書店發行

4 · The Progressive Movement

Our age possesses a much greater number of component parts; their mechanical and dynamic properties are also new. And the skeleton of their constitution (assembled to fulfil new tasks) must be made in a new form.

El Lissitzky, 1920

The broad cultural and artistic developments brought about by the May Fourth Movement, as well as the creative climate inspired by the 1917 Russian Revolution, continued to hold significant appeal for Chinese designers through the Thirties. With the collapse of the Qing dynasty two important preoccupations emerged that were to have a direct bearing on visual design during this period. The first was an intense desire for political self-determination and the recovery of a sense of national identity that had been stripped away by a series of military defeats and territorial concessions. The second was the recognition of the need for new technology and increased modernization that would restore China to its rightful place as a world power. Both of these are frequent themes in Chinese graphic design of the Thirties as it evolved from a practice of passively informing to a profession more demonstrably persuasive and socially engaged.

The call by reformers to study Western geometry and mathematics as a means of moving China further into the 20th century was instrumental in defining a new set of aesthetic forms. With equal diligence, designers began to explore the possibilities of a visual language capable of communicating the ideals of a new, rational society. Working with abstract symbols, linear construction and broad colour planes, graphic designers hoped to bring a new sense of logic and structure to their work. The introduction of simplified typographic forms was of particular interest for designers exploring the functional potential of the character. Similar to the sans-serif letter forms of the West, a new range of Chinese characters was developed, highlighting the beauty and simplicity of their geometric components. With this emerging desire to lend

Above: Creation Monthly, *1928. Publisher: Shanghai Creation Society.*

Opposite: Literature, *October 1933. Editor: The Literary Association, with Lu Xun. Designer: Chen Zhi-fo. Publisher: Shanghai Life Book Store. 26.5 x 19.0 cm.*

Ladies' Monthly, *1933. Publisher: Shanghai Ladies' Book Store. 21.5 x 15.2 cm.*

order and clarity to the growing number of designs competing for attention, visual hierarchies were also introduced in both advertising and publication design to give precedence to information by its degree of importance. Titles were given the most prominent role in establishing a compositional order. In addition, the frequent use of large numerals for graphic identification of an issue number became popular with many magazines, while the standardization of mastheads and other graphic elements helped achieve easy recognition amongst a magazine's readership.

Inherent in the idea of a new technological society was the preoccupation with construction. While modern modes of transportation and industrial machinery became frequent visual themes of this period, the concept of 'building' was deeply embedded in the design process itself. The works of the Progressive Movement are the first to explore the actual techniques of graphic construction for its functional value. With the development and implementation of an underlying grid or framework, designers began to redefine, with systematic precision, the division of pictorial space. Concepts of symmetry and balance, which dominated the works of the Twenties, also underwent serious re-evaluation and the introduction of the Golden Mean encouraged a better proportional relationship of visual components.

These new-found geometric techniques of graphic construction can also be traced to a renewed interest in traditional architectural forms. Both architectural ornamentation and decorative pattern had long been recognized as essential components of Chinese daily life. From the simple lattice designs found in the most common of homes to the more elaborate designs found in pagodas and temples, geometric decoration has enriched the Chinese landscape for centuries and carried with it built-in meaning. In part, these concerns for the introduction of vernacular influences came from the earlier lessons of Lu Xun and his insistence that Chinese design should speak from its own experience. In the Art Deco influences of the Shanghai Style, such themes also played an important role for their purely decorative quality. The inclusion of repetitive patterns reminiscent of classical textiles or architectural motifs added in turn another dimension to the compositions of this period. While implicitly suggesting their Chinese origin, the use of graphic patterning also recalled the underlying structure of the works. The cumulative advantage of these techniques for the designers of the Progressive Movement was their profound ability to communicate, through symbolic images and geometric forms, a composite picture of a book or magazine's contents.

Working from a method first developed during the 10th–12th centuries, Chinese designers also explored the theoretical manipulation of eye level

Far left: The Ark, *February 1935. Publisher: The Ark Press, Mid-China Printing Company, Tianjin.*

Left: Xing Zhong Monthly (*Developing China Monthly*), *June 1937. Special issue on national defence. Designer: Qian Jun-tao. Publisher: Xing Zhong Monthly Association, Shanghai. 26.0 x 18.5 cm.*

within a composition. With this technique early artists had succeeded in uniting images of unrelated distances and horizons in perfect detail without bowing to the scale restraints of Western perspective. Through similar means many designers from the Progressive period devised a casual shifting of vantage points which succeeded in comfortably juxtaposing images of unrelated sizes for a new dynamic appeal. Furthermore, it was thought that a work free of horizon lines and perspective offered new possibilities for the free circulation of the eye and an unrestricted opportunity for the viewer to enter the picture plane from any angle. This was of paramount importance, as designers of the Progressive Movement tried to free the viewer from the many routine habits of seeing that prevented them from truly comprehending a design's message.

During the Twenties photography had also succeeded in gaining a prominent place within the fine arts in China. Numerous weekly and monthly journals were founded to supply technical information about the latest equipment, as well as to provide a place for reproducing recent photographic achievements. Initial forays into photography had only produced conventional scenes of landscape and still life as if viewed by a classically trained painter: the potential of the camera remained relatively unexplored.

By the Thirties, however, directions in photography had begun to change and the medium was soon welcomed as the ideal means for communicating the

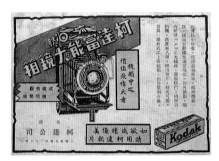

The Eastman Kodak Company was one of the first photographic enterprises to advertise and distribute its range of products in China. Top left: *Advertisement for No. 620 Kodak large-format camera, c.1930.* Above: *Artist's self-portrait, using Kodak camera, 1930s.*

Right: *Advertisement for Mirror Box, 1937. Designer: Zheng Yue-bo.*

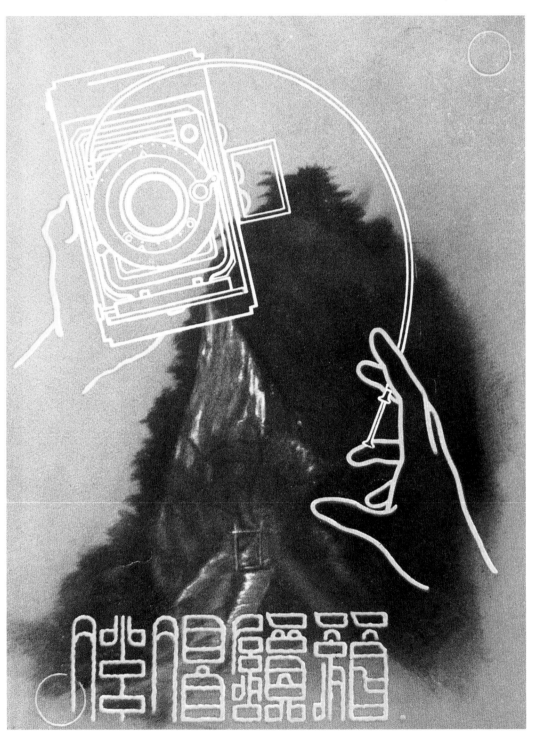

visions of the modern age. While immensely popular among the urban Chinese in the foreign districts, photography was still widely reviled as a form of black magic in the neighbouring countryside where superstition reigned. Demonstrations of the camera's capabilities in rural villages often spurred hostilities on the part of their citizenry, resulting in the loss of equipment or destruction of the photographer's home. For graphic designers, nevertheless, the camera offered a seemingly unlimited number of new possibilities for creativity and communication.

Three Association Book Store, Shenyang, 1930s.

Throughout the Thirties the ideas formulated by designers of the Progressive Movement were further explored by photographers who felt that the implicit realism of their medium lent an important degree of credibility to their subjects. Until this period little attention had been paid to the documentation of daily life. Instead, photographers usually chose subjects that were closer to the traditions of the fine arts, such as portraiture, still life, landscape and nature studies. This lack of interest in the more common images of life was in part due to the bulky nature of the equipment used, but it also reflected the mass taste of the period which still emphasized traditional beauty. With the advent of the Progressive Movement, however, photographers began to employ new visual techniques to reorientate the picture plane similar to those used in purely graphic compositions.

Particular attention was given to images that depicted a physically strong and technologically advanced China. Photographs devoted to the glorification of the human body engaged in competition or sport became commonplace. Shot from angles which heightened the drama of the event or isolated as a single frozen moment through the technique of collage, such preocccupations with human performance signalled, like a gear in the overall machine, the importance of the individual in the transformation of society.

Such varied and often complex approaches to art and design as developed in the Progressive Movement were seen as necessary preconditions to the changing of engrained cultural preconceptions. Indeed, it was thought that only through the complete restructuring of visual symbolism towards a purer modernist vision could the socially engaged designers of the period succeed in eliminating all remnants of China's feudal past. In retrospect, what the artists and designers of the Progressive Movement were proposing was a total transformation of art and design – and with it the ultimate liberation of the Chinese spirit.

The New Voice of Typography

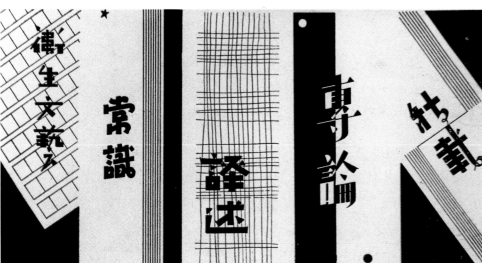

The Thirties were hailed as a period of advanced communications and increased mechanization. With the number of advertisements and visual messages bombarding the public now reaching an all-time high, designers of the Progressive Movement introduced new techniques for the ordering of graphic information. The resulting reorientation of the picture plane signalled a radical departure from previous methods of graphic composition. The use of new typographical forms and geometric abstraction on book covers, magazines, advertisements and posters reiterated the flexible potential of the Chinese character and its ability to communicate emotionally as well as symbolically. Texts began to be accorded a place within a composition based on their degree of importance and visual strength. With the combined use of geometric shapes and graphic lines, the designers hoped to create new, dynamic compositions that would overcome people's tired habits of reading and bring new expression and meaning to a written message.

To underscore the enormous potential for a new graphic dynamism based solely on type and structure, consider the unique properties of the Chinese language, which allow lines of text to be composed either vertically or horizontally, and from left to right or right to left. The freedom this allowed designers for visual experimentation helped to break down the many conventions inherited from earlier Western-inspired compositions, and led to a fuller exploration of the Chinese language for its unique design potential.

Top left: Ladies' Monthly, *1933. Publisher: Shanghai Ladies' Book Store. 21.5 x 15.2 cm.*

Top right: Literature Weekly, *undated special issue on Russian short stories. Designer: Qian Jun-tao. Publisher: Shanghai Kaiming Book Store.*

Above: *New literature advertisement, c. 1937. Designer: Zhang Xue-fu.*

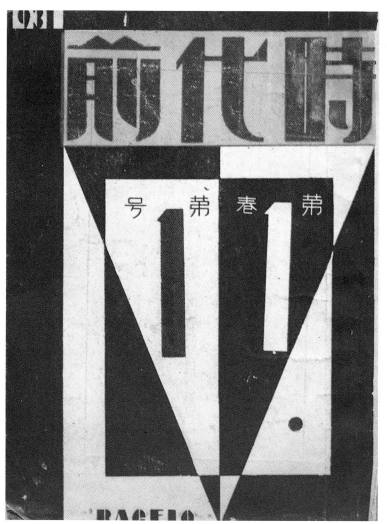

Ahead of the Times, *January 1931. Designer:*
Qian Jun-tao. Publisher: Ahead of the Times
Magazine Association, Shanghai. 20.3 x 15.3 cm.

Modern Woman, *1933. Designer: Qian*
Jun-tao. Publisher: Shanghai Guanghua Book Store.

The New Voice of Typography

The book designs of Qian Jun-tao demonstrate a highly developed interplay of geometric structures and textual hierarchies. After being a major force in the development of Chinese graphic design during the Twenties, Qian began to symbolize the gradual evolution toward graphic functionalism, witnessed in the designs of the Progressive Movement during the Thirties. His expert handling of typographic styles and linear components, as in his design *Ten Years of the Shenshi Telegraphic Dispatch Agency*, is a credit to his remarkable versatility, and was instrumental in the development of the early Progressive style.

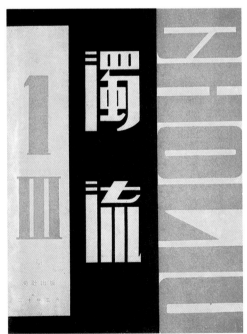

Top left: Shanghai Private Kaiming Correspondence School, Members' Club Quarterly, *No. 5, c. 1930. Designer: Qian Jun-tao. Publisher: Shanghai Kaiming Book Store.*

Top right: Shanghai Private Kaiming Correspondence School, Members' Club Quarterly, *No. 6, c. 1930. Designer: Qian Jun-tao. Publisher: Shanghai Kaiming Book Store.*

Bottom left: Going Where?, *1930. Designer: Qian Jun-tao. Publisher: Shanghai Shuimo Book Store.*

Bottom right: The Muddy Stream, *1931. Designer: Qian Jun-tao. Publisher: Zhuo Press.*

Ten Years of the Shenshi Telegraphic Dispatch Agency, *c. 1930. Designer: Qian Jun-tao. Publisher: Shanghai Sishe Press.*

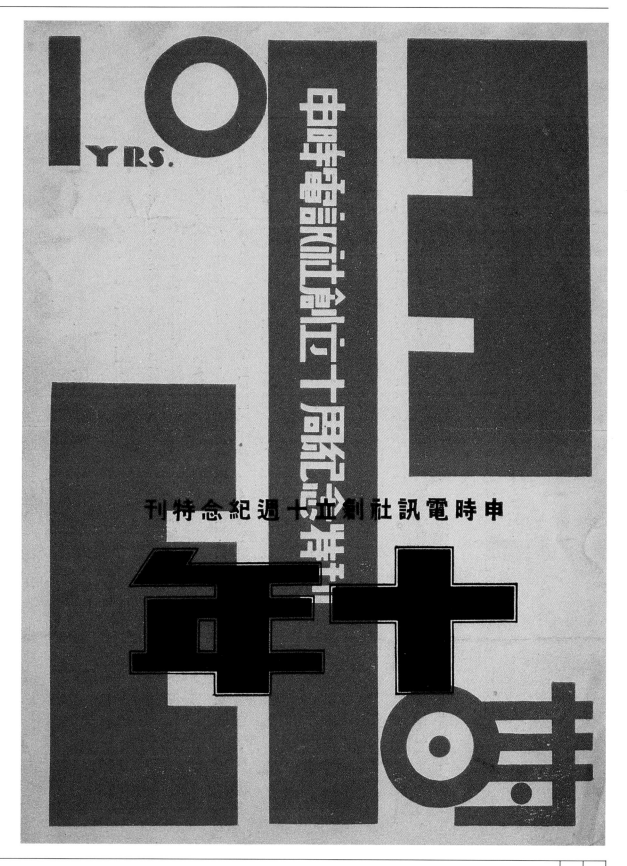

Design and the Machine

The rationality of the machine appealed to designers of the Progressive Movement, who sought to define their changing environment through a new visual logic. In China, technology and the advancing machine age were seen by many as a form of salvation and in the designs of the Progressive Movement they were often idolized as such. Ranging from mechanized travel to new methods of industrial production, depictions of the machine symbolized its popular role as the greatest hope for the modernization of China's backward lifestyles.

For designers, these interests were expressed in two ways. On the one hand, images of imaginary machine components, such as gears and turbines, metal housings and rivets, all provided new subject matter from which to base cover designs for a recent influx of technical and scientific journals. On the other hand, the actual process of thinking and designing was itself affected by a similar form of aesthetic rationalism.

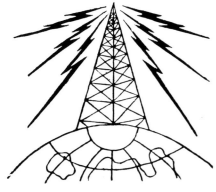

無線電

飛艇商標

理工雜誌

第 一 卷
第 二 期

震旦大學
理工學院發刊
土山灣印書館印

Designers of book and magazine covers began to concern themselves with theories of reductive functionalism. Gone were the stylish excesses of the Shanghai Style, which had been little concerned with design as a conceptual process.

Far left: Science and Engineering Magazine, *1935. Designer: Hong Qing. Publisher: Zhendan University College of Science and Engineering Press. 26.0 x 18.5 cm.*

Above left: New Times Monthly, *1933. Publisher: Shanghai New Times Press. 26.0 x 19.0 cm.*

Above: *Trademarks for a radio broadcasting company, c. 1930 (top) and for Jiangtai Bread and Biscuit Manufacturer, Shanghai, 1931.*

Right: Science and Engineering Magazine, *1935. Designer: Hong Qing. Publisher: Zhendan University College of Science and Engineering Press. 26.0 x 18.5 cm.*

Dynamic Photography of the Progressive Movement

By the Thirties numerous examples of photographs from the Russian avant-garde had made their way to the cosmopolitan centres of China and were providing inspiration for a new generation of socially and politically engaged photographers. To emphasize their visions of a modern China and the glory of its social and technological advances, photographers of the Progressive Movement sought to document their environment from new angles, thereby re-examining what might otherwise have passed as mundane. The Chinese works of this period were greatly influenced by European photographers and by the Russian Constructivist Alexander Rodchenko, who believed that the camera should work as a tool to disclose new facts about one's daily reality. Chinese photographers resolved that their medium should play an active role in the transformation of society. Their collaboration with the graphic designers of the Progressive Movement helped create compositions that broke with the academic

Far left: The Central China Monthly, *1934. Publisher: The Central China Monthly Publishing Office, Shanghai. 32.2 x 24.5 cm.*

Above left: The Ark, *back cover advertisement, August 1937. Publisher: The Ark Press, Mid-China Printing Company, Tianjin.*

Above: Ladies' Life, *1936. Publisher: Shanghai Life Book Store. 22.0 x 15.0 cm.*

Above right: Pictorial Weekly, *1933. 'Excellent Works of French Photography'. Publisher: Chinese Photography Association, Shanghai. 18.5 x 13.3 cm.*

Pictorial Weekly, *September 1935. Publisher: Chinese Photography Association, Shanghai. 18.5 x 13.3 cm.*

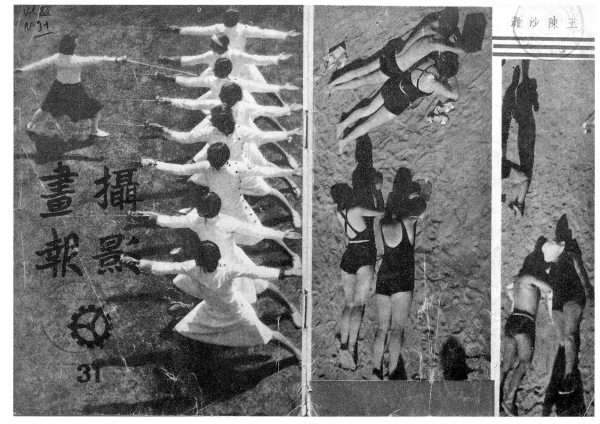

Dynamic Photography of the Progressive Movement

traditions of the past. Photographs of the human figure were frequently shot from below to show the towering strength of the individual, while images of street demonstrations were often taken from above to accentuate further the unity and force of a people united in rally. Of particular interest at this time were images that also expressed the inherent linear and geometric forms of the industrial environment. Once again using unusual camera angles and vantage point, photographs of bridges and construction sites that might otherwise have been viewed as routine building projects became instead glorified monuments to a modern China.

Left: The Central China Monthly, *1934.Publisher: The Central China Monthly Publishing Office, Shanghai. 32.2 x 24.5 cm.*

Above: Modern Miscellany, *1930. Photographer: Wang Yu-kui. Publisher: China Art Press.*

The Growth of Photographic Societies

During the early Thirties Shanghai saw the development of at least three major photographic societies devoted to exploring photography as an art. 'The Black and White Society' was composed of artists of middle-class origins; 'The Society for the Study of Photography' had a primarily upper-class membership; and finally 'The Flower Group' consisted of many older and established photographers. To join an association photographers were usually required to gain the support of several existing members, as well as to submit a representative portfolio of photographs for review. In addition, they were expected to pay an annual membership fee which helped to offset the costs of a yearly exhibition and its related publicity. On occasion a catalogue was produced in conjunction with the exhibition and additional funds were raised through the sale of advertising on the back pages.

Left: The Artery of Society, *1948.*
Photographer: Mu Yi-long. From: The China Focus.
Publisher: Tianpeng Art Association, Shanghai.

Below: River Bank, *1928. Photographer: Chen Wei-zhuang. From: The China Focus. Publisher: Tianpeng Art Association, Shanghai.*

The Ark 1935–37

By 1935 *The Ark* began to show a radical change in both its editorial content and aesthetic design. Perhaps drawn into a confrontation with the readily changing literary and artistic currents of the period, the magazine developed a remarkably liberal literary tone and became a leader of the Progressive design style. Suddenly taking on a complex visual character. *The Ark* began to use often startling, highly experimental photography which juxtaposed images of contrasting scales with a new body of playful graphic markings. The introduction of photographic screens and coloured overprinting constituted an entirely new approach for Chinese graphic design and broke with the conventions of traditional publishing which, until this time, had tended to place single representative images on its magazine covers.

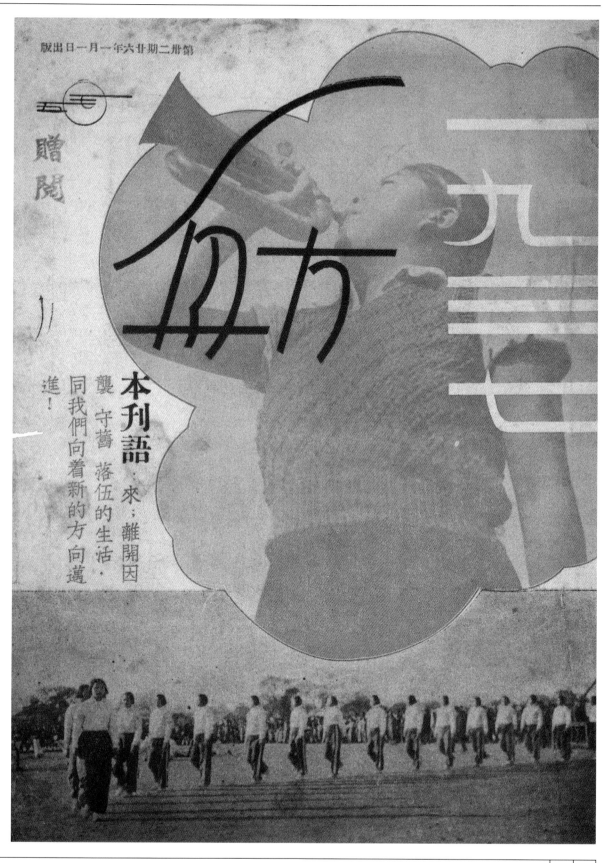

Far left: The Ark, *August 1937*. Publisher: *The Ark Press, Mid-China Printing Company, Tianjin.*

Left: The Ark, *June 1936*. Publisher: *The Ark Press, Mid-China Printing Company, Tianjin.*

Right: The Ark, *January 1937*. Publisher: *The Ark Press, Mid-China Printing Company, Tianjin.*

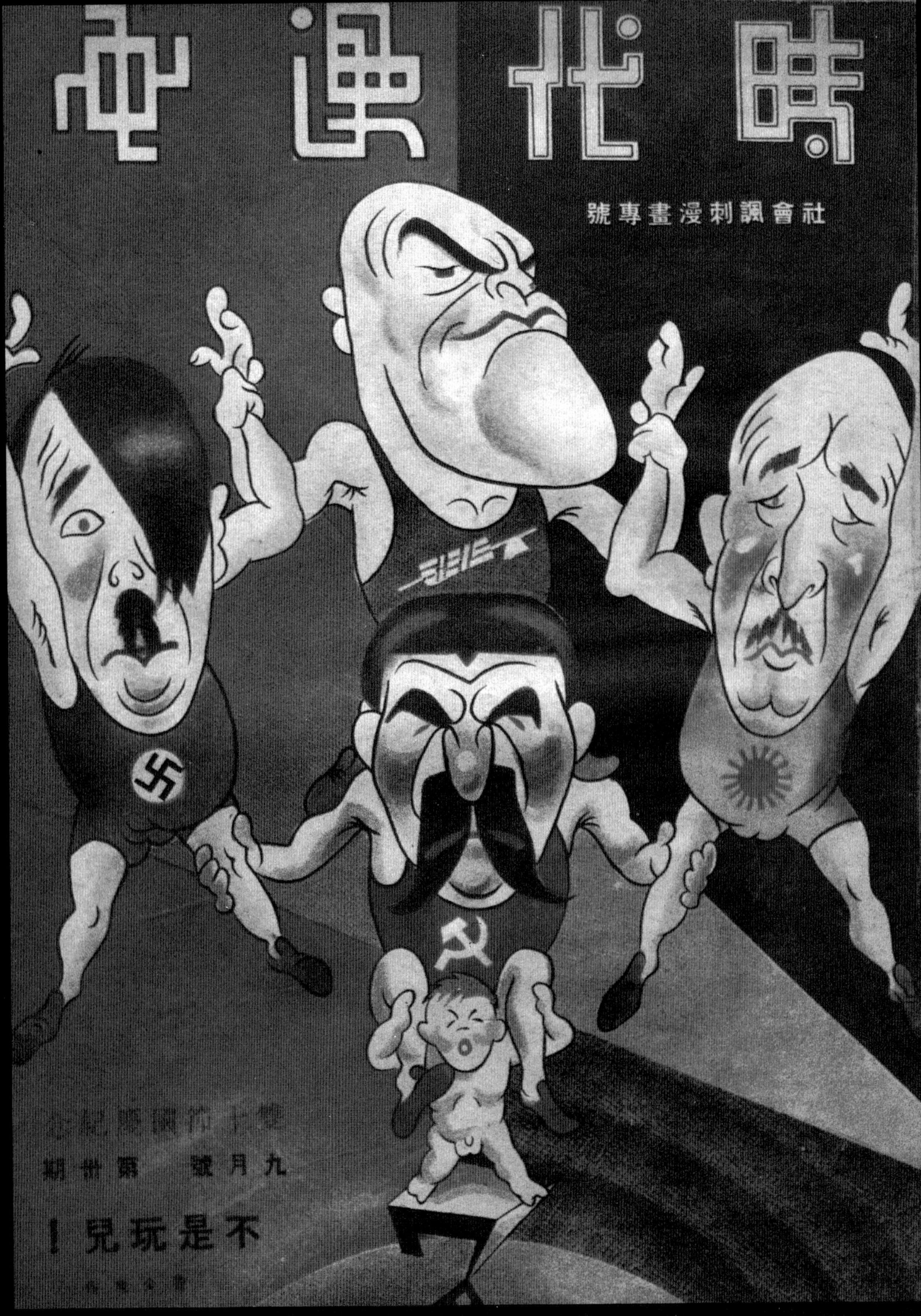

時代漫畫
社會諷刺漫畫專號
雙十節國慶紀念
九月號 第卅期
不是玩兒！

5 · Proletarians and Paper Tigers

Above: Military Magazine, *August 1936.*
Students in European Military Research.
*Editor and publisher: Military Magazine Association
of the Military Committee, Nanjing.* 22.3 x 15.2 cm.

Opposite: Modern Sketch, *September 1936.* It's
not fun. *Illustrator: Lu Shao-fei. Publisher:
Shanghai Modern Publications.*

*I have said that all the reputedly powerful reactionaries are merely paper tigers. The reason is that they are
divorced from the people.*
Mao Ze-dong, speech at the Moscow Meeting of
Communist and Workers' Parties, 1957

In response to the ongoing debates about China's future the Communist Party began organizing left-wing artistic associations during the 1930s. Its goal was to attract individuals who had been sympathetic to the May Fourth Movement by stressing the Party's commitment to a broad range of contemporary social problems. Interest in such associations grew following Japan's invasion of north-east China in 1931 and the subsequent bombing of Shanghai in 1932. Both these events brought renewed signs of nationalism and questions were raised about China's ability to respond in a cohesive and forceful manner.

With this new wave of Japanese incursions, numerous organizations and businesses began to call for an end to trade with Japan and a boycott of all Japanese goods. This action eventually led to the mounting of an official 'War of Resistance to Japan'. In the mid-1930s Chinese products began to display labels identifying them as such and asked customers to avoid foreign brands. Frequent stories were told of shopkeepers who, in an attempt to sell their Japanese stock, placed newly printed Chinese labels over the originals to disguise their origin.

The often ambiguous affection that the Guomindang government maintained for foreign governments, particularly Nazi Germany and Fascist Italy, led to further assaults by leftist artists whose sympathies favoured the younger, more proletarian Communist movement. As Chiang Kai-shek displayed an increased interest in dictatorial control, intellectuals began to question the direction of domestic policy and sought to expose high-level corruption. Their self-adopted roles as watchdogs signalled a new willingness on the part of artists and writers to become more directly involved in the fabric of China's political system.

Removing signs advertising Japanese products during the 'War of Resistance to Japan', Shanghai, 1938.

By 1937 Shanghai had become a stronghold for both political and cultural reform. With popular support for artistic and literary journals reaching new heights, many magazines sought to address the nation's problems through biting criticism of the national leadership and unpopular foreign influences. As a result, bold expressions of contempt were not only directed at the Japanese but any country whose culture or values were seen as antithetical to Chinese interests. Satirical journals grew in number and employed a new generation of illustrators to create images laced with political and cultural commentary. Caricature played a major role in the new illustration techniques of this period, with well-known foreign personalities frequently rendered in savage form. Precedents for this style of magazine can be traced to the years immediately after the fall of the Qing dynasty, when a taste for satirical social novels and scandal fiction grew out of disillusionment with Yuan Shi-kai's republican government. In general these works appealed to the reading public by presuming to uncover cases of corruption and abuses of official power. Much to the delight of readers, no sector of the nation was exempt from the roving pens of the writers as they sought out wrong-doing in business, education, religion and even journalism itself. Through such techniques of satire and caricature artists solidly advanced the role of visual and literary commentary to create images both forceful and direct.

During this period, the art of caricature was also adopted by mobile 'propaganda teams'. First founded in Shanghai in 1937, such teams aimed at helping the rural population understand the meaning of the 'Anti-Japanese' and 'Rescue China' movements. Establishing close ties with workers' associations, the propaganda teams used large-scale posters and murals to illustrate unfair labour practices, poor working conditions and corrupt management. Travelling from village to village, they sought out local opera and theatre troupes with which to work. Believing that their messages would be better understood if played out through the local folk idiom, the propaganda teams often combined their graphic images with street peformances to animate further their subjects. It was not unusual for such groups to play before 20,000 people or more in a day, thus making this form of mobile media an effective means of mass communication. With similar groups dispatched to work with peasants' associations, many new members were enlisted to oversee the process of land reform during the coming years. As Mao joyously exclaimed: 'that such political propaganda could spread throughout the countryside is due to the Chinese Communist Party and peasants' associations. With only simple slogans, pictures and lectures, it seems that the peasants have gone through political colleges. That is indeed very effective.'

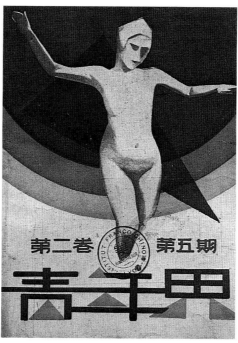

As a further step in promoting their cause, many caricature propaganda teams worked directly with editorial staffs to form national magazines such as *Anti-war Caricature* and *China Sketch*. Such collaborations were not limited to peasants and workers, however. The formation of a variety of artistic and literary associations also helped to unify creative and intellectual dissent in the cities. With the regular support and encouragement of the newly formed Communist party, similar associations were also fundamental in promoting such magazines as *The World of Youth*, *The Students' Magazine* and *The Juvenile Student* – all of which catered to a young, reform-minded readership. While such publications were important for introducing Marxist theory, many were also respected for their open support of the numerous worker and peasant uprisings that were sweeping the country. Well illustrated with political cartoons, diagrams and caricatures, these journals were appealing to China's youth in addition for their general mix of subjects, from popular science to politics.

As land-reform policies were introduced in the Communist-held liberated territories, artists across China began to depict the awakening of the peasant classes. Few magazines were exempt from this shift in the portrayal of Chinese society. Where once designers and illustrators had focused on the growing urban middle class and their affection for imported products and foreign styles, there now came a barrage of images depicting the liberation of the Chinese

Above left: The Bloodshed of Workers in Beijing and Shanghai, *May 1923. Editor: Beijing Workers' Weekly Magazine Association. Publisher: Beijing-Shanghai Railway, Shanghai Office. 18.6 x 13.0 cm.*

Above centre: The World of Youth, *December 1932. Designer: Zheng Shen-qi. Publisher: Shanghai Beixin Book Company. 21.2 x 15.3 cm.*

Above: The Students' Magazine, *May 1923. Publisher: Shanghai Commercial Press. 24.7 x 17.5 cm.*

Above left: China Sketch, *December 1936.*
Designer: Tian Wu-zai. Publisher: China
Publication.

Above right: China Sketch, *December 1936.*
The End of Science *(back cover). Illustrator: Ai*
Zhong-xin. Publisher: China Publication.

nation. Particularly significant advances were also made with regard to the representation of women. Magazines such as *The Cosmopolitan* began to concentrate more on themes of personal independence and a rejection of feudal courtship and marriage practices. Other images signalled an end to landlord exploitation and economic inequities which had for centuries kept peasants toiling for subsistence wages. Illustrations in newspapers and journals began to describe in detail the horrifying economic conditions and living standards in the remaining areas of Guomindang-controlled China as the Nationalist government bled the countryside of its natural resources and food supplies.

The Chinese press and the artists and writers who had been raised on the May Fourth ideals began to speak out with a new sense of urgency, in whatever way was available to them, in hope of making significant changes in the lives of the Chinese people. Many of the artists and writers were subjected to censorship, persecution or imprisonment and because of this the journals were often shortlived. But as the portrayals of daily life evolved, so did public opinion. Thus came a realization of the great social and political potential of art and design to create meaningful change. While for some it may have seemed that things would simply continue along their current course, the seeds of indignation and a growing commitment to change had taken root. The many individuals who were responsible for this period of soul-searching soon found that they had unleashed a tide of human determination that would prove fundamental in bringing about one of the most significant revolutions in modern history. As a consequence, the role of art and design would also undergo a radical change: ceasing to cater to private interests, it would work to define a new social and political order that would last for the next thirty years.

Below left: The Liberation Daily, *Yan'an, 1943.* By Comparison. *Illustrator: Gu Yuan. The quality of life during the famine in Henan Province – and in the liberated areas.*

Below: Military Magazine, *April 1937. Editor and publisher: Military Magazine Association of the Military Committee, Nanjing. 22.3 x 15.2 cm.*

Caricature and the Satirical Journal

The notion of satire in Chinese art can be traced back to the Eastern Han period (AD 25–220) when it was first used to depict a ruthless and dictatorial emperor. In the Ming dynasty (AD 1368–1644) artists began to render the lives of the physically deformed as a means of illustrating everyday social injustice and personal hardship. By the late 19th century, foreign influence from such diverse artists as Goya, Daumier and Beardsley had helped to revive both interest and credibility in caricature art, further inspiring its development.

A resurgence of interest in caricature and satire during the 20th century developed as a result of a growing split in China's domestic politics. Between 1927 and 1937 the widespread persecution by the Guomindang government of artists and writers associated with left-wing cultural associations, popularized by Lu Xun, had reached alarming proportions. Political coercion was widely used to limit the printing of progressive journals and many liberal bookstores were closed indefinitely.

Under the relative protection of Shanghai's foreign concessions, a new generation of illustrators sought to expose these blatant abuses of official power and stem the rise of human injustice. Between 1934 and 1937 Shanghai saw the development of over 20 different journals devoted solely to caricature art. The magazines *Modern Sketch*, *China Sketch*, *Caricature Life* and *World Knowledge* thus became vehicles of popular resistance and reform. While most were shortlived (*Modern Sketch* had the longest life, surviving three years and 39 issues), they proved immensely popular for their witty essays, depictions of local life and inventive poems.

The earliest cover illustrations were humorous commentaries on the adaptation of Chinese men and women to the many changing social roles around them. With time, more emotional renderings of China's growing economic inequalities highlighted the severe poverty of millions of Chinese and provided crucial support for rural reform. The War with Japan was also a regular topic for illustrators and new questions were raised about the government's support for a growing number of dictatorial leaders around the world.

While actual print runs for each magazine rarely exceeded 10,000 copies, the nature of the material guaranteed a broad circulation; each copy was passed amongst family and friends. Such habits effectively raised the exposure of the caricature journals by three or four times the original publication figure and brought with them broader public condemnation of the country's ills. Continual attempts by the government to shut the journals took their toll, but the significant advances made in the art of caricature showed once again that graphic imagery could be far more effective than words alone.

Caricature Life, *September 1934. 'Screaming for Life'. Illustrator: Huang Shi-ying. Publisher: Shanghai Art and Life Publications.*
26.2 x 19.3 cm.

China Sketch, *November 1935. Illustrator: Chen Zhen. Publisher: China Publication.*
26.0 x 19.0 cm.

Top left: World Knowledge, *February 1926. 'The Tragedy of the Japanese Parliament'. Illustrator: Chen Yi-fan. Publisher: Shanghai Life Book Store. 25.8 x 18.8 cm.*

Top right: World Knowledge, *March 1926. 'Japan was intoxicated by the Fascist Wine'. Illustrator: Chen Yi-fan. Publisher: Shanghai Life Book Store. 25.8 x 18.8 cm.*

Bottom left: World Knowledge, *July 1926. 'North China in the Mouth of a Volcano'. Illustrator: Chen Yi-fan. Publisher: Shanghai Life Book Store. 25.8 x 18.8 cm.*

Bottom right: World Knowledge, *August 1926. 'Striking at the Invaders'. Illustrator: Chen Yi-fan. Publisher: Shanghai Life Book Store. 25.8 x 18.8 cm.*

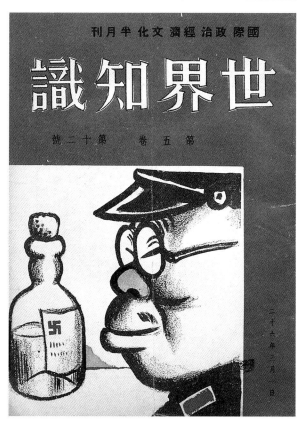

Caricature and the Satirical Journal

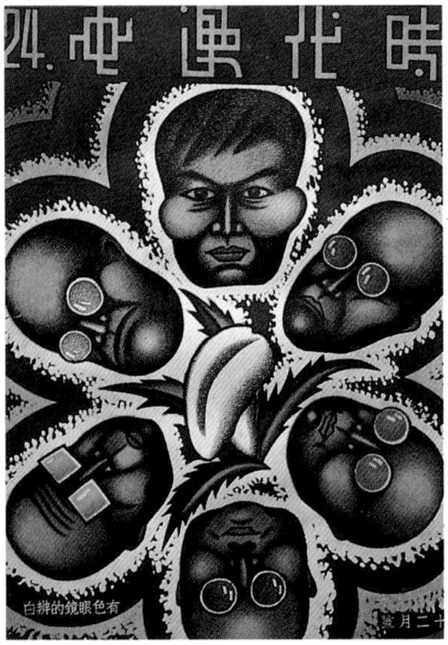

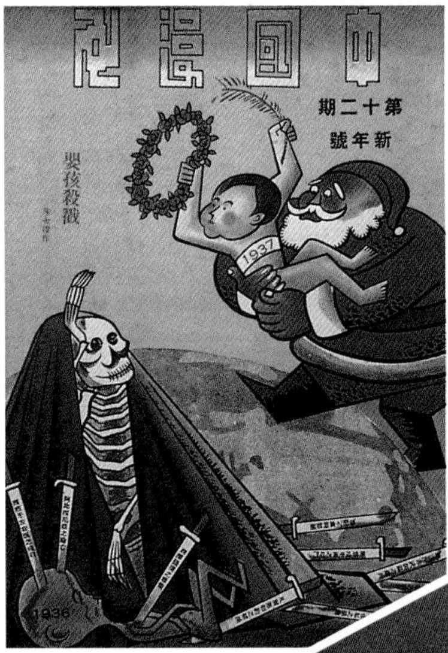

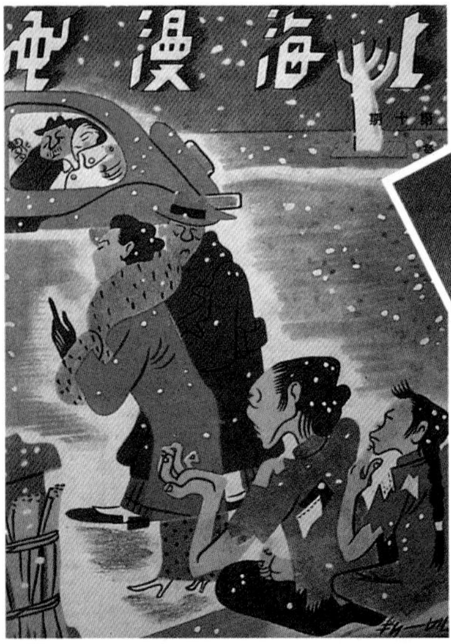

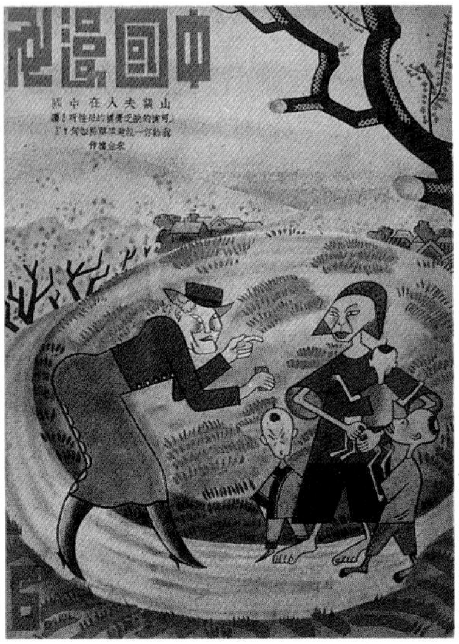

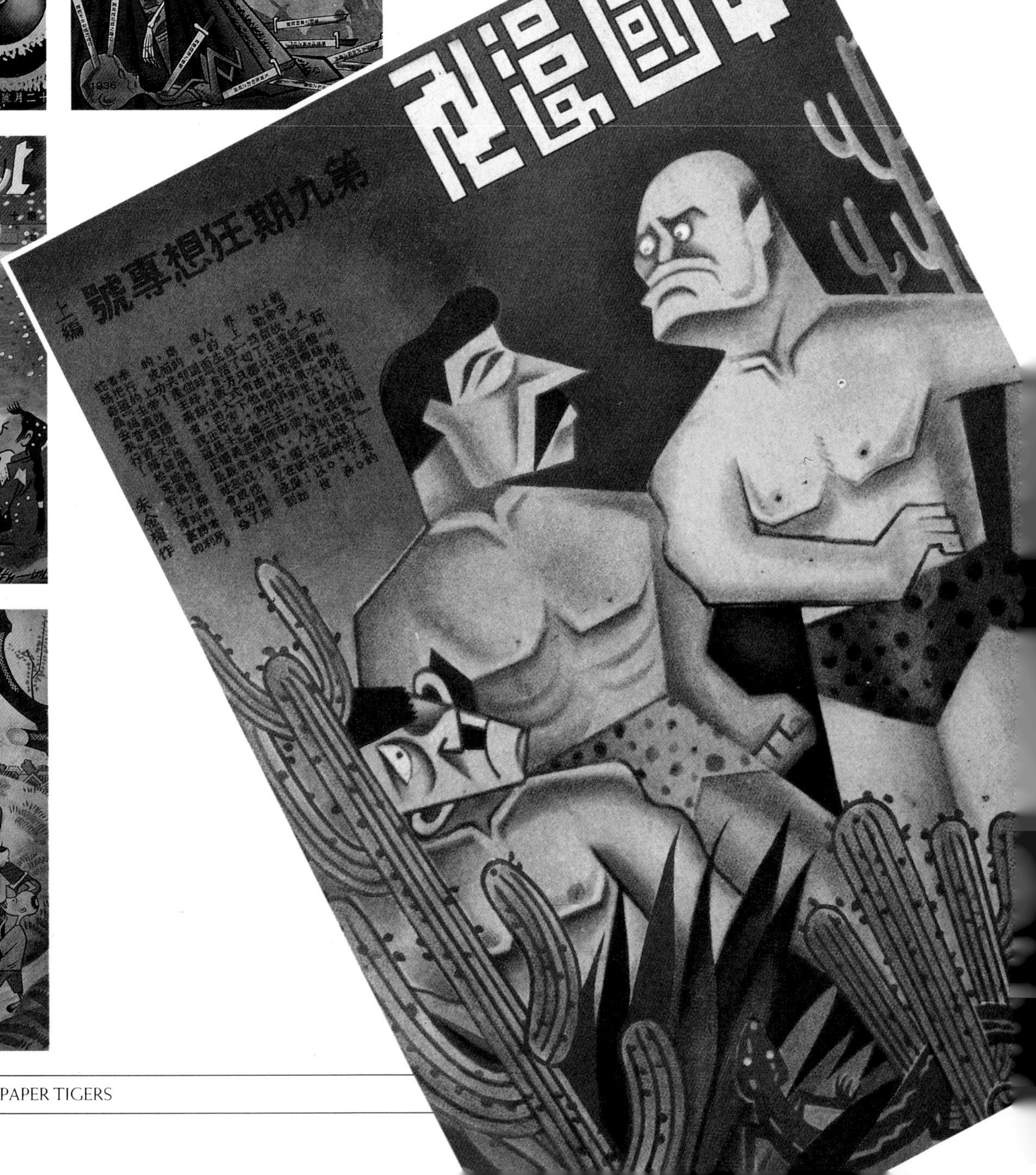

Far left, top to bottom: Modern Sketch, *November 1935. Publisher: Shanghai Modern Publications. 25.7 x 18.8 cm.*
Shanghai Sketch, *March 1937. Illustrator: Yan Zhe-xi. Publisher: The Independence Press, Shanghai. 26.3 x 19.0 cm.*
China Sketch, *April 1936. 'Madame Sanger in China'. (Margaret Sanger was an American proponent of birth control.) Illustrator: Zhu Jin-lou. Publisher: China Publication. 26.0 x 19.0 cm.*

Top left: China Sketch, *January 1937. Santa Claus delivers a new child into a world of violence and death. Illustrator: Zhu Jin-lou. Publisher: China Publication. 26.0 x 19.0 cm.*

Left: China Sketch, *October 1936. Mussolini, Stalin and Hitler meet in the wild. Illustrator: Zhu Jin-lou. Publisher: China Publication. 26.0 x 19.0 cm.*

Right: China Sketch, *November 1936. China as a sleeping giant. 'Give me Liberty or Death.' Illustrator: Li Xuan. Publisher: China Publication. 26.0 x 19.0 cm.*

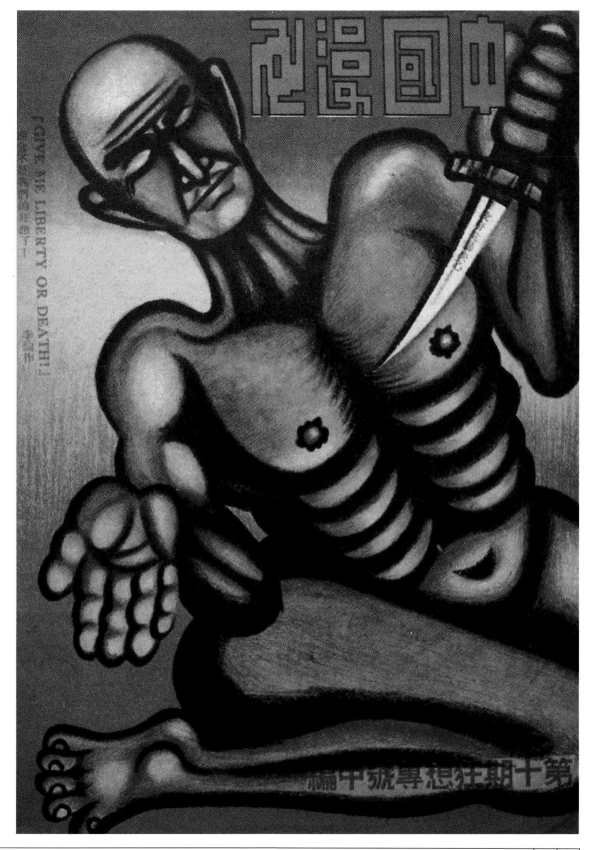

The Immediacy of Montage

The development of photomontage techniques for creating social and political satire corresponds to other forms of Chinese photographic experimentation that were widely embraced during the mid-Thirties. The growing crisis in domestic politics and an economy on the verge of collapse brought widespread criticism from China's intellectuals. Illustrators and designers previously unconcerned with politics became overnight activists by diverting their creative talents to the making of harsh visual critiques of China's sorry state of affairs. Common themes were the Japanese invasion of northern China, the corruption of society by Western influences and the soaring rate of inflation. Artists and designers, who were hesitant to be identified for fear of reprisal, were allowed a degree of anonymity by working with photographs clipped from popular journals. Following in the footsteps of the European Dadaists Hannah Höch and Raoul Hausmann, these new photographic satirists quickly discovered the ability of juxtaposed images to create powerful, often highly emotional commentaries. Unlike the time-consuming techniques of illustration and caricature, the method of photomontage required no more than a pair of scissors and a pot of glue, but brought with it the inherent visual advantages stemming from realism and plausibility.

Above left: The Material City and the Bankrupt Village, *1934. Photomontage. Artist: Luo Gu-sun.*

Above right: Assorted Pictures from the North, *1934. Photomontage. Artist: Feng Zi-li.*

A Typical Chinese,
1936. Photomontage.

時代漫畫社製

標準中國人

The Changing Image of Women

Bombarded by the influx of Western ideas and living in a society with rapidly changing cultural values, women in Chinese society probably underwent more change between 1911 and 1949 than in all previous centuries. By 1920 the widespread use of foot binding, which had served to immobilize women for hundreds of years, had been reduced to a practice found only in the most remote provinces. Similarly, the traditions of forced marriages and the giving of child brides had been denounced as feudal practices that reflected badly on China's move towards modernization. Private industry succeeded in drawing large numbers of women into the workplace, and the resulting increase in expendable income and available commodities had the effect of creating a consumer class of women for the first time in Chinese history.

While all of these changes made women targets for new forms of exploitation, particularly in the realms of ready-to-wear fashions and cosmetics, a growing interest in the New Literature had the very positive effect of diminishing the Confucian values popularized in Mandarin Duck and Butterfly fiction. The resulting preoccupation with modern themes helped to expose many of the inequities of the past. Specialized magazines began to address issues of particular concern to their female audience; filled with articles on education, the changing domestic scene and opportunities outside the home, such magazines explored a variety of alternatives for the modern woman. They regularly featured photographs and short essays by and about women from all walks of life, as well as paintings and illustrations by aspiring women artists. By 1934 Shanghai had witnessed the establishment of the Women's Commercial & Savings Bank, in addition to a variety of other services which were run by and catered to the needs and wishes of an exclusively female clientele.

Far left: The Ladies' Journal, *January 1929. Publisher: Shanghai Commercial Press. 26.4 x 19.0 cm.*

Left: Violet, *June 1930. Illustrator: Hang Zhi-ying. Publisher: Shanghai Dadong Book Company. 21.0 x 15.0 cm.*

Above: Modern Miscellany, *1930. Publisher: China Art Press.*

Opposite left: The Ladies' Journal, *March 1929. Publisher: Shanghai Women's Magazine Company. 26.4 x 19.0 cm.*

Opposite right: The Woman's Pictorial, *April 1934. Designer: Guo Jian-ying. Publisher: The Liang You Printing and Publishing Co. Ltd. 26.5 x 19.0 cm.*

The late Thirties brought continued changes in illustrated representations of women. Magazines that had previously shown them as vulnerable, dependent and self-absorbed began to introduce designs that stressed their great inner courage, physical resilience and moral strength. Images portraying women as isolated or solitary now began to depict more active sporting and social lives, either in the company of men or groups of other women.

In time, even the seemingly progressive illustrations of modern urban couples began a shift toward sharper, more realistic representations, often excluding the man entirely. A revival of interest in the plight of rural women caught in the grips of backward and repressive traditions also provided new subject matter for artists and drew attention to proletarian themes. The image of self-sufficiency in the face of hardship became a symbol for the Chinese woman and further

inspired memorable illustrations of an integrity, dignity and personal sacrifice that had long gone unrecognized.

By the mid-Forties women had become a well-documented part of China's national liberation effort by taking active roles in the new Red Army. Mao Ze-dong had openly welcomed women to the revolutionary base at Yan'an and praised them for their work in introducing successfully new role models of capability and equality.

Opposite: The Cosmopolitan, *April 1934* (far left) *and May 1934* (left). *Illustrator: Tao Yun. Publisher: Shanghai Cosmopolitan Press.*

Above: The Cosmopolitan, *November 1933* (top) *and February 1934* (above). *Publisher: Shanghai Cosmopolitan Press.*

Right: Graphic Pictorial, *August 1946. Publisher: Graphic Pictorial Book Company.*

6 · Yan'an and the Artistic Ideal

As for revolutionary popular literature and art, it is especially important that it begin by making use of the simple proletarian street vernacular.

Qu Qiu-bai, 1934

As Mao Ze-dong began to solidify his power in the mountainous army base of Yan'an he was quick to recognize the need for an effective visual langauge for the dissemination of the Chinese Communist Party's (CPCs) philosophy. Formed in response to politically complex objectives and an illiterate rural population, a distinct aesthetic philosophy began to emerge, drawing heavily on regional folk design traditions. Techniques of papercut and minority painting were carefully observed for their intrinsic ability to communicate through the popular idiom, then mixed with the necessary political ideology to form hybrid statements of great simplicity and force. Foremost in the mind of Mao was the belief that art should not exist for purely artistic reasons, but rather that it should serve both political and ideological ends.

In plain contrast to this new Yan'an philosophy was the still prevalent cosmopolitan view of art and design, highly attuned to commerce and Shanghai's progressive urban tastes. The developments of these styles, as we have noted previously, was in part a result of the domination of the foreign treaty zones, as well as of the 1919 May Fourth activities. Artists who had been born and trained in the more cosmopolitan areas had relatively little contact with what they must have felt were China's more backward and remote provinces. Consequently, the emerging Yan'an style initially held little appeal for most of these individuals. Nonetheless, motivated by a sense of national urgency and an idealistic spirit, many younger artists from the eastern coastal areas of China travelled to Yan'an to join the Communist-led resistance efforts. There they met other writers and artists to form work teams which were further to develop this new interrelationship between politics, art and society.

Opposite: Bombing the Bunker, c.1940. Woodblock. Illustrator: Gu Yuan.

Above left: *Students of the Lu Xun Academy engaged in group exercises, c.1943, and the abandoned church they used as meeting hall and performance centre.*

Above right: Two Generations, *c.1940. Woodcut. Illustrator: Li Hua.*

Widely acclaimed as the forerunner of the new Yan'an artistic objectives, Lu Xun and his populist ideas were enthusiastically embraced by the Communist leadership. In his honour the Lu Xun Academy of Literature and Art (often refered to as Luyi) was formed in a Catholic church in Yan'an, based on the belief that studies in theatre, music, literature and fine art would serve to organize and educate the masses. The training in each of these areas was broad and tended toward an interdisciplinary approach, with each department often incorporating aspects of the others. The fine arts department, in particular, developed a broad curriculum including courses in drawing, propaganda painting, caricature, printmaking and the history of art, as well as philosophy, sociology and Marxist ideology. While there was no tuition, students at the academy were required to perform agricultural labours and in exchange they were provided with food and clothing. The ultimate results of these exercises in self-sufficiency were the valuable contacts the students were able to establish with the local peasants, whom they used as models for their studies.

For many students this rather spartan rural life was a continual test of endurance. Materials and equipment were in short supply, thus challenging each pupil's ingenuity. As a natural response to the unfamiliarity of their surroundings, the students set about recording the lifestyles of the peasants and environment around them. In so doing, they produced the first of many such

images of labour that would become commonplace in years to come with the intensive rebuilding of the Chinese economy. Many of the works produced by the students also took on a secondary role, for they were regularly circulated amongst the peasants with the appropriate Chinese characters clearly marked beside the objects or animals featured. In this way, the inhabitants of the neighbouring villages were slowly taught to read.

The growing interest in the artistic merits and communicative potential of woodblock printing was primarily due to the earlier teachings of Lu Xun. As we have seen, the Chinese had perfected both the visual and technical development of woodcut by as early as the Song dynasty (AD 960–1279), but Lu Xun gave it contemporary relevance. The first exhibition of modern Chinese woodcuts was held in Shanghai in 1931, to be followed by a highly influential travelling exhibition mounted in 1936. Both shows focused extensively on contemporary social and political issues, particularly scenes of peasant life, labourers in factories and urban working-class districts. The dominance of proletarian themes was partially inspired by European and Soviet examples. The artists Kirchner, Kollwitz and Frans Masereel were especially influential for their emotional depictions of man's struggles against cruelty.

The first of many mobile woodcut groups was formed in 1938 by artists from the Lu Xun Academy. Unimpeded by bad weather and difficult terrain the

Above, clockwise: Autumn Harvest, c.1940. Illustrator: Gu Yuan. Drawing class, Lu Xun Academy, 1942. Lu Xun (left) at the first national travelling woodcut exhibition, October 1936. Logo of the Research Association for Modern Creative Woodblock Printing, 1940s.

Above: *Writers and artists at Mao Ze-dong's Yan'an Forum on Literature and Art, 1942.*

Right: Mediating a Marriage, *1943. Woodblock. Illustrator: Gu Yuan.*

groups circulated through the neighbouring mountains, creating numerous images expounding on the horrors of the Japanese occupation, thus implementing an ideological war of resistance. By the early Forties travelling artists were also engaged in the documentation of peasants struggling to overcome centuries of feudalism and exploitation through the introduction of new land reform policies. The portability of woodblock printing was ideally suited to the clandestine nature of this work; artists could produce and distribute unlimited copies of their designs with relative ease. For this reason woodblock became an ideal medium for the dissemination of ideological messages and was seen as a prime means of inducing both political and social change.

In 1942 a forum for artists and writers was convened in Yan'an with the explicit intent of examining the relationship between art and revolutionary society. The meeting was significant, bringing together diverse artists and intellectuals to debate such topics as the alienation of the artist in society, class consciousness, assimilation and integration. It was during this period that Mao came to define more clearly the theoretical differences between Yan'an and the May Fourth Movement, as well as the tenets of Chinese socialist art in general. In his key address *The Yan'an Forum on Literature and Art* Mao encouraged artists to reject the direct and unquestioning importation of foreign images in favour of a genuine artistic language responsive to China's own condition and people. He believed the notion of art for art's sake to be a bourgeois concept and a luxury that held little meaning for the majority of China's population, since it failed to contribute concrete ideas to the pressing social and economic problems of the day. In his words, art should use 'the rich, lively language of the masses' in order to move beyond its select urban audience and live up to its primary responsibility of communicating to the people.

Knowing that Chinese artists would benefit by exposure to a valid alternative to the influx of predominately Western aesthetics, cultural representatives of the CPC were dispatched to Moscow to study Soviet propaganda methods and their implementation. In seeking Moscow's assistance Mao hoped to secure an effective propaganda model for use in the cities, where sophisticated tastes and a higher standard of living made people suspicious of the Communists' intentions.

During the late Forties artistic themes often centred on the harmonious relationship between peasants and soldiers. Images of the People's Liberation Army (PLA) assisting the peasants in their annual harvests and arbitrating local disputes became commonplace and helped to attract new recruits and ensure broad public support. By the time of the Chinese Revolution in 1949 the popular arts of Yan'an had proved effective in transforming large portions of the largely illiterate rural population. With only slight stylistic and theoretical modifications to the original Yan'an principles, the government of Mao Zedong was to rely heavily on the talents of artists and designers for the next two decades as they embarked on a long course of national reconstruction and attempted to move China further into the 20th century.

Above: The Lu Xun Academy of Art and Literature, 1940. Illustrator: Gu Yuan (self-portrait).

Left: Designs for paper money, 1942 (far left) and 1944 (left). Illustrators: Shen Rou-jian and Wu Yun.

The Influence of Chinese Papercuts

Papercut, Shaanxi Province.

The rural people of China have long engaged in a variety of artistic expressions that offer key insights into both the routines of their daily lives as well as their celebrations. While only recently elevated to the level of nationally recognized art forms, the traditions of such works are ancient and grow out of the unique characteristics of China's many minority cultures. The intrinsic need to celebrate and communicate the joys and sorrows of life have produced a broad range of expressive folk arts, many of which remain largely undocumented.

Perhaps the best-known examples of Chinese folk art are the intricate papercuts that grace the windows of simple homes during the spring festival. Most play a totemic role by protecting the household from evil spirits or helping to cure or expel illness. Others serve as fertility symbols and are used at weddings. Visually striking and often complex in design, papercuts have long been admired and collected in the West for their intricately cut forms. The obvious lack of concern for scale or perspective gives them a highly stylized appearance and suggests an innate and unfettered sense of design. By tradition, Chinese papercuts never seek a realistic representation of a subject, but remain the interpretative visions of the individual artists, inspired by their own combination of religion, superstition and regional folk tales.

Right: -Cat papercut, Qingyang, Gansu Province.
Artist: Zhang Xiu-zhen.

Ox papercut, Ansai, Shaanxi Province. Artist: Gao Jin'ai.

Deer papercut, Ansai, Shaanxi Province. Artist: Cao Tian-xiang.

Good luck papercut for doorway, Yanchang, Shaanxi Province. Artist: Liu Lan-ying.

Below: Tiger papercut, Ansai, Shaanxi Province. Artist: Chen Sheng-lan.

Images of Struggle, Visions of Change

The constant exposure of the art students and teachers at the Lu Xun Academy to the papercuts made in the nearby villages had a major effect on their sense of design and helped them develop a better understanding of the peasants' daily struggle to survive. Through a recognition of the enormous narrative potential of these simplified interpretations of life, the Yan'an artists began to create similar images of daily rural life mixed with the themes of modern education and changing social roles.

Most important to the revolutionary printmaking movement were Gu Yuan and Li Qun. Both artists were deeply committed to the future of China and the role that art would have in the education and liberation of its people. Their bold woodblock prints are particularly notable examples of the images produced at the Lu Xun Academy. Intent on depicting the hardships of peasant life, both artists sought to expose the feudal customs and backward thinking that created China's impoverished conditions. Their documentation of the land reform movement, advances in education and the liberation of women helped bring the inspiration fundamental to meaningful change.

The artist Li Hua, while not a member of the Yan'an community, was also important in the popularization of woodblock in the rural areas. Focusing almost entirely on the themes of peasant life and the country's prolonged civil war, Li became well known for his ability to render emotive themes with tremendous voracity and strength. His sympathy for the peasants and hostility to the forces that kept them bound to the soil became a major artistic preoccupation during his lifetime. With a studied interest in facial expressions and human anatomy, Li Hua created images of physical intensity rarely matched by his contemporaries.

Left: Meeting for the Reduction of Rent, *1944. Woodblock. Illustrator: Gu Yuan.*

Above: Teaching New Midwifery, *c. 1940. Woodcut. Illustrator: Gu Yuan.*

Above: Portrait of Lu Xun, *1936. Woodcut. Illustrator: Li Qun.*

Right: Women from the Red Army helping to repair a Spinning Wheel, *1945. Woodcut. Illustrator: Li Qun.*

Above: Down with Imperialism!, *1936. Woodcut. Illustrator: Li Hua.*

Right: Struggling to Survive, *1947. Woodcut. Illustrator: Li Hua.*

The Emergence of a Mass Revolutionary Style

The aesthetic guidelines to emerge from Mao's Yan'an Forum on Literature and the Arts in 1942 fuelled new attempts to produce a mass revolutionary design style. Initial forays suggested the importance that woodblock and the imported tastes of Soviet Socialist Realism would play. Magazines such as *The World* and *The Enlightened Teens* are prime examples of designs meant to symbolize a growing national interest in social and political themes. With the only reference for a revolutionary Chinese art being that of woodcut, illustrators continued the traditional peasant themes explored by artists from the Lu Xun Academy. In an important attempt to appeal to a broader, more literate readership, however, the drawing styles showed a gradual move away from the simplistic lessons of the rural propaganda groups. An increased sense of illustrative drama heightened the urban appeal of these themes, and began to attract a new audience to the plight of China's peasant people.

By 1949 and the proven success of the revolution, illustrated book and magazine covers had adopted a new tone of security and began to feature illustrations of a proletarian work force engaged in the rebuilding of the Chinese economy. Other images focused on the hope of China's youth, as children in minority costumes joined hands in anticipation of their new futures. The illustrations of this period remained largely realistic portrayals of China's land and its people.

Below: The World, *October 1947. Publisher: The World Press.*

Opposite, top to bottom: The Enlightened Teens, *September, October, November, December 1949. Designer: Ke Yang. Publisher: Shanghai Kaiming Book Store.*

Far right: The Enlightened Teens, *February 1950. Designer: Wu Yun. Publisher: Shanghai Kaiming Book Store.*

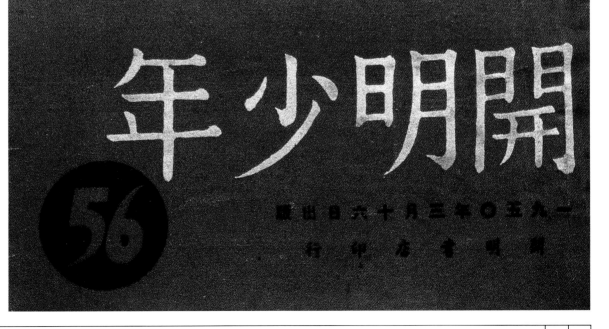

7 · The Revolutionary Machine

In the world today all culture, all literature and art belong to definite classes and are geared to definite political lines. There is in fact no such thing as art for art's sake, art that stands above classes, art that is detached from or independent of politics. Proletarian literature and art are a part of the whole proletarian revolutionary cause; they are, as Lenin said, cogs and wheels in the whole revolutionary machine.
Mao Ze-dong, *Talks at the Yan'an Forum on Literature and Art,* May 1942

Like the Emperors of China before them, the new Communist leaders felt that it was their responsibility to shape the cultural development of the nation. It was their belief that no political revolution could be truly successful if it was not simultaneously accompanied by cultural reform. To maintain the values of the previous capitalist and feudalist systems would be incompatible with the goal of a revolutionary transformation of society and would undermine China's effort to move its people into a period of modernization.

It became increasingly evident in the early years of the new government that the obstacles in the way of the transformation of Chinese society were numerous. The country had not only been severely torn by a prolonged civil war, but was divided by its own geographic regions, class structures, ethnic groups and languages. In addition, party cadres who were more often chosen for their political prowess than for their education were often at a loss in the cities when dealing with the intellectual and artistic establishments that had their roots in the May Fourth Movement. For this reason, commissions were more often granted to those artists with whom they shared a Yan'an past, rather than to artists with a Shanghai background. This brought about charges of cronyism and prejudice, accompanied by the recognition that much was yet to be done to heal the very evident differences between the Yan'an and Shanghai philosophies.

In time, three central themes emerged from top-level discussions on the arts. These included the need to develop and implement a mass national culture, to unify the relationship between the Party, artist and audience and finally to tackle the division between the Yan'an and Shanghai artistic traditions. As with

Opposite: Hai Xia, *c. 1960. Cinema poster. Designer: Xu Xin.*

all decisions affecting China's new course, it was Mao Ze-dong who formulated the party's basic artistic and cultural doctrines. His particular belief about art was that 'the more artistic it is, the more harm it can do the people and the more it should be rejected'. Just as Constructivist art and design was eventually denounced by the Communist leadership in Russia, the Chinese found it difficult to trust the political correctness of works too complex for untrained party cadres to understand. For this reason it was determined that art should seek the broadest aesthetic denominator for reaching the greatest number of people while serving the cause of socialist reconstruction.

In July 1949 the National Congress of Artists and Writers was held in Beijing. This was the first national gathering of its kind since Mao's Yan'an Forum on Literature and Art in 1942. It was here that decisions were made that would affect the creative arts in China for the next decade. Seeing the independence of their work falling prey to the dictates of party politics, many artists attending the congress sought compromises that would allow them to retain a degree of aesthetic flexibility. Suggestions were made for the approval of a hybrid style which would merge the ideological strength of Yan'an with the technical and visual advances of the Shanghai Style.

By the early Fifties, however, it was apparent that such a compromise would be unacceptable. The beginning of the Korean War in June 1950 had the effect of excluding completely the already minimal foreign influence entering China and the Party establishment quickly moved to eliminate what it viewed as a bourgeois May Fourth artistic heritage. In most respects this signalled the end of the expressive Shanghai traditions that had been fundamental to the development of graphic design during the previous three decades.

As Western influence vanished, the Chinese authorities began to fill the growing artistic void with works loosely based on the Soviet socialist realism that they had been exploring since the Forties. Concentrating on representations of idealized social and political models, artists recently trained in the Soviet Union returned to create works solely devoted to the proletarian struggle. This introduction of new aesthetic priorities clearly constituted a major break from the more individualistic and stylish images of the past, though the underlying tenets of socialist realism were not unfamiliar to the Chinese. The portrayal of 'heroic figures', for example, had an historical precedent in earlier Chinese literature. Given the predilection for such mythical representation, the works now being introduced were to find an element of cultural validity. Eventually filtered through Mao's Yan'an vision, a socialist realism of a more distinctly Chinese kind was formed, blending a high degree of representation with obvious references to both folkloric and rural traditions. The effect of this

Share the Labour and Share the Fruit, *1957. Poster. Designer: Cai Zhen-hua.*

共同劳动 · 共享成果

integration was to make the new art more appealing to the masses while garnering support for the political line. Although the techniques of illustration would vary over the next twenty-five years, the basic formula remained relatively unchanged until Mao's death in 1976.

In May 1956, in an effort to rally China's intellectuals to his support, Mao announced a new mass movement called the Hundred Flowers Campaign, with its title taken from his statement 'Let a hundred flowers bloom and a hundred schools of thought contend'. With this pronouncement he sought to build the confidence of those who had felt their creative contributions stifled or undervalued in previous years. The initial reaction was understandably cautious and by early 1957 there was only nominal response to his call for openness and criticism.

In order to reassure Party officials worried about any large amount of criticism, Mao delivered in February 1957 his now well-known speech 'On the Correct Handling of Contradictions Among the People', in which he stated that only through creative struggle and education can the ideal of socialist construction advance. By the late spring of 1957 a thaw was being felt in China's artistic and intellectual communities and Mao's promise to protect creative freedom while opening the party to criticism was finally met with an outpouring of artistic and literary works in an attempt to recapture some of the spirit of the May Fourth Movement of the Twenties. At the same time, there was a small resurgence of the Shanghai tradition itself, an attempt to reinvigorate art and design with a broader, less xenophobic approach to creativity. Spawned by the apparently sincere interests of Mao Ze-dong, through his repeated calls for openness, government criticism, political actions, strikes and worker unrest suddenly rose to alarming proportions and threatened to destabilize the country.

Because of the speed and intensity with which the Hundred Flowers movement departed from its intended course, Mao was forced to take serious action by reversing the campaign he himself had initiated. In late June 1957 the movement came to an official end and was quickly superseded by a major counter-revolutionary campaign.

Branded as 'rightists' in reference to their supposedly threatening anti-government and anti-revolutionary stance, artists, writers and intellectuals became easy targets for persecution. Only recently encouraged to speak out about the creative and theoretical questions that concerned them, those who had been the most outspoken or had shown an interest in experimentation were harassed, humiliated, demoted or jailed. Artists who managed to survive the frequent interrogations and criticisms were often abandoned by their families,

who considered them outcasts and wished to avoid aspersions that could easily hinder them in their professional lives for years to come. The resulting ruination of lives and depletion of creative talent, as well as the totally inhibiting creative climate during this period, took a heavy toll on the visual arts.

Nevertheless, during the period 1949 to 1966, artists who followed the political line were involved in a wide variety of health, science and economic modernization drives. The scale and importance of artistic involvement in publishing and mass mobilization initiatives were also unsurpassed and led to the government's continuing recognition of the ultimate potential for art and design to educate and motivate the people effectively.

With further ideological plans waiting to be put into action, designers again lent their considerable talents to realizing a comprehensive course of economic restructuring and modernization. Since 1949 there had been remarkable advances toward the building of a substantial industrial base, and Mao Ze-dong set his sights on the further development of heavy industry and agriculture. The key element in this plan was Mao's belief that the country's greatest resource was its enormous population, including 500 million peasants, most of whom he viewed as under-utilized. The subsequent mobilization of human resources, which became known as the 'Great Leap Forward', relied heavily on

Government-sponsored education and health campaigns sometimes took on an entirely unpredicted momentum. The drive by a quarter of the world's population to 'Eliminate the Four Pests' led to a concern that the natural ecological balance of the country's food chain would be upset.

Above left: Propaganda performance team, Nanjing, 1956. Above top: Waving flags and banging pots drives a frightened sparrow population close to extinction. Above: Propaganda group, Ningbo. Such groups were modelled partly on Russian agitprop techniques, but were also a natural outgrowth of China's own tradition of itinerant operatic, theatrical and storytelling troupes.

New Chinese Women, *April 1954.*
Photographers: Lang Qi and Yang Ji-ping.
Publishers: New Chinese Women Association. 25.5 x
18.0 cm.

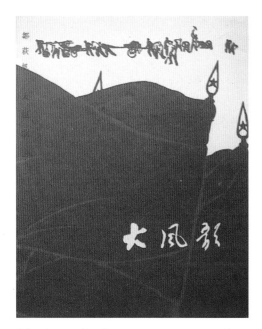

The Song of Dafeng, *1961. Designer: Liu Cheng-*
yin. Publisher: The Writer's Publishing House.

visions of ideological and political propriety in its attempt to motivate the people. With the slogan of 'more, faster, better and cheaper' the party hoped to lead a rapid transformation of the nation and narrow the widening social and economic gap between the cities and countryside. Focused on raising China's GNP to a level comparable to those of other industrialized nations within fifteen years, the Great Leap became a feverish movement of local production cooperatives and constituted the most extensive Chinese propaganda campaign to date.

While the early years of reconstruction relied heavily on photography to illustrate happy individuals engaged in building and agriculture, the period 1958–59 saw the rapid introduction of new, highly exuberant illustrative techniques. Where once the realism of photography had been used to document with great credibility successes in harvesting and construction, it was not the ideal medium for the creation of expressive and compelling imagery that would mobilize the nation. For this reason, artists were quick to find an alternative medium in which to portray the lofty ideals of the Great Leap. This was achieved through the introduction of a new and dynamic illustrative style, by which yearly production goals were emblazoned on brilliantly coloured banners and symbolic monuments. Thereby, the movement achieved a degree of idealization, far removed from the rather mundane reality of raw-material drives and backyard smelting furnaces. The importance of this creative decision should not be underestimated, for it set a precedent not only for an important illustrative style that photography could not match, but simultaneously raised the level of motivational graphics to a higher conceptual level, a technique that was to be repeated during the Cultural Revolution.

By the early Sixties a split could be felt in the party thinking as Mao came under attack for the devastating failure of the Great Leap Forward and his plan for collectivization. Numerous individuals within the Communist leadership also began to recognize the need for a realistic compromise on its strict aesthetic views. Artists had been encouraged to adhere to a narrowly defined socialist-realist model, only creating works that portrayed class struggle and the revolutionary ideal. The Yan'an principle – that art should serve workers, peasants and soldiers – was slowly broadened to reflect a more moderate stance. With this loosening came a new degree of artistic innovation. In 1962 Zhou Yang, then the Minister of Culture and Propaganda, suggested that artists and writers portray a more authentic picture of what he termed 'middle characters'. This would include the recognition of human error and one's own shortcomings, thus breaching the longstanding drive for representations of purity and the heroic character.

A key part of this liberalizing climate must also be attributed to Premier Zhou En-lai, who seriously reviewed the problems inherent in the earlier definitions of 'acceptable art'. In doing so, he came to realize the stultifying effects of years of arbitrary criticism levelled by party cadres with little or no training in the visual arts. As a result Zhou sought some nominal degree of freedom for artists and openly stated that only by freely exploring their creative interests would artists and intellectuals be able to make authentic contributions to China's development. The effect of Zhou's efforts was enough to encourage many demoralized artists and intellectuals to begin a renewed exploration of their artistic potential. It was at this time that a second 'Hundred Flowers' began to blossom, with designers once again engaged in stretching their talents to contribute their impressions of a new and often visionary image of China's future. In particular, Qin Wei and Li Zhong-yun opened a new frontier for the imagination with their cover designs for *Popular Science*.

In many ways the period 1962–65 began to resemble that of China in the Fifties as the country came to enjoy a new calm. With both agriculture and industry steadily recovering from major setbacks and with commendable improvements made in the areas of housing, education and healthcare, all signs pointed to a general recovery. While the number of students entering the arts had dropped significantly since 1949, those who now held positions in design and illustration found a renewed, albeit temporary, degree of satisfaction. Only with the first hints of the coming Cultural Revolution was this calm broken: no one could have predicted the scale of devastation and personal loss that the next ten years would bring.

Above left: Go all out, aim high and achieve a complete victory, *1961. Poster. Illustrator: Weng Yi-zhi.*

Above right: Popular Science, *1963. Illustrator: Qin Wei. Publisher: Popular Science Press.*

Destroy the Old and Establish the New

In 1958 Mao Ze-dong introduced the modernization programme known as 'the Great Leap Forward', which required the mass mobilization of the Chinese people. In order to accomplish this gargantuan feat the government turned to individual artists, as well as peasant and worker art associations, for contributions that would constitute a nationwide media campaign. Cultural policymakers envisioned an art that would further Mao's goal of uniting 'revolutionary realism with revolutionary romanticism'. As a Chinese initiative, the concept of combining realism with romanticism had the effect of loosening the Soviet grip on art and design of the period while expanding the range of indigenous artistic styles. Authorities hoped this move would appeal to artists and particularly encouraged reference to China's own literary and artistic past, thus giving art and design a more authentic pedigree. As a result, images of the time take on strongly idealistic and heroic themes depicting the unity of the people engaged in a myriad of agricultural and industrial developments.

Posters and magazines were prime formats for communicating these new objectives, for they could be easily circulated and displayed in the workplace. Artists, encouraged to portray China's abundant and happy workforce engaged in modernization, rendered a wide array of locations, including hospitals, factories and power stations. The slogan 'Walk on two legs' frequently appeared, encouraging the people to work for technological advancement by using ingenuity when faced with a scarcity of raw material. Numerous posters were also designed with children in mind, representing them as the glory of China's future, fully immersed in the studies and labours that would make the nation strong. While today these designs are often ridiculed as facile and transparent forms of propaganda, they were remarkably effective during this period for their ability to inspire and motivate Chinese society. Such images lent encouragement to the nation and brought to the workplace a genuine and uplifting spirit of group co-operation. Through the thousands of portrayals of people united in national reconstruction, new links were forged between the masses, the party and a unique brand of artistic expression.

Far left: Father likes Work and I like Work also, *May 1960. Illustrator: Chen Ju-xian. Publisher: Shanghai People's Fine Arts Publishing House.*

Left: A Peasant Woman Yesterday: A Productive Expert Today, *1960. Illustrator: Zhao Jing-dong. Publisher: Tianjin Publishing House.*

Below: Guarding the Peace is a Hero, Constructing the Motherland is a True Man, c. *1958. Poster. Illustrators: Ha Qiong-wen, Yang Wen-xiu, Qian Da-xin, Weng Yi-zhi.*

Pride in Production

The results of China's first Five Year Plan for economic restructuring, introduced in 1953, were hailed as an overwhelming success, with industrial increases reaching an average of 18 per cent per year. The production of steel alone had more than tripled, while coal and electrical output had both doubled. For the years 1958 to 1962 a second economic drive was introduced, devoting more attention to agricultural development. In a feverishly organized plan to accelerate production, the slogan raise 'more, faster, better and cheaper' was introduced through hundreds of graphic posters, and massive agricultural communes were formed to pool available land, equipment and human resources.

To provide increased incentives and to celebrate the monthly advances under the communal system, a new illustration style was developed, symbolizing the massive effort under way. Posters and magazines all boasted dream-like images of glorious harvests emblazoned with large numerical records of the tremendous increases in production. Groups of peasants, hunched from the weight of their bounty, hoisted monumental buckets of grain amidst bursts of fireworks to celebrate their remarkable achievements. Not to be outdone, steel workers and factory employees were also shown gallantly parading with their manufactured wares to underscore their own national records.

The ability of these images to motivate the people appeared remarkably promising when, by the end of 1958, government statisticians began to boast of a doubling of agricultural output. Within the next six months, however, these claims would be proved inaccurate, for it was discovered that peasants around the country, so excited by the prospect of achieving the annual goals and receiving the recognition and fanfare assured by the colourful posters around them, had grossly misreported their real production figures. From this point onward, government propaganda specialists acknowledged the ability of graphic posters to raise the spirits and enthusiasm of the country's work force, but also recognized the misleading effect of advance publication of production figures.

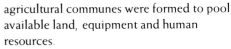

Left: New Industry and Commerce, *No. 17, 1958. Publisher: New Industry and Commerce, Bimonthly Press. 26.0 x 18.5 cm.*

Top: Shanghai Industry and Commerce, *October 1958. Publisher: Shanghai Industry and Commerce, Bimonthly Press. 26.0 x 18.5 cm.*

Above: New Industry and Commerce, *No. 15, 1958. Publisher: New Industry and Commerce, Bimonthly Press. 26.0 x 18.5 cm.*

Right: Shanghai Industry and Commerce, *July 1958. 'Leap Forward together under the Flag of the General Line.' Illustrator: Wu Hua. Publisher: Shanghai Industry and Commerce, Bimonthly Press. 26.0 x 18.5 cm.*

The Development of a Revolutionary Folk Art

Through the late Fifties, designers were readily encouraged to return to the inspiration offered by the Chinese folk art traditions first recognized and implemented in Yan'an. Actual authenticity was not required, but simply creating a folk-inspired likeness proved to be enough to satisfy aesthetically untrained cadres. Used on posters and in magazines, illustrative techniques derived from papercuts and peasant paintings were thought by government officals to be effective for their ability to motivate the people through the use of a familiar visual language. Most depicted harmonious scenes of an idealized peasant life and incorporated simple political slogans encouraging collective labour and collective reward or recalled some previous agricultural achievement. They were aesthetic and conceptual precursors to a style later to be resurrected during the Cultural Revolution. Meantime, the wholesale diversion of artistic talent during the coming years for the creation of this mythical culture had an extremely damaging effect on the arts.

In many cases rural artists who, prior to this renewal of official interest, were able to withstand the influences of modernization and political upheaval, were subjected to a re-training process. On a national scale the attempt to bring art education to the peasants had the unfortunate effect of obliterating many of China's authentic minority and folk traditions.

New Industry and Commerce, No. 15, 1958. Advertisement. 'The Flowers of the Great Leap'. Illustrators: Zhuang Ping and Zhang He-ming. Publisher: New Industry and Commerce Bimonthly Press. 26.0 x 18.5 cm.

Four Modernizations – Achieved Earlier: An Abundant Harvest of All Food Crops, *January 1960. Poster. Artists: Central Academy of Fine Arts Painting Department. Publisher: Shanghai People's Fine Arts Publishing House.*

Foster the Flowers of the Nation, *May 1960. Designer: Fan De-kang. Publisher: Jiangxi People's Publishing House.*

A Period of Creative Calm

The first half of the Sixties brought a brief renewal of artistic freedom and creative innovation. Divisions within the Party following the disaster of Mao's Great Leap Forward and a period of natural calamities were accompanied by a serious re-thinking of official artistic objectives. Many leaders had begun to question the value of such massive outlays of human energy and life and suggested that the physical and emotional costs were not proportionate to the level of economic return.

As a consequence, the loosening of official controls on artists and a general atmosphere of moderation and calm helped to encourage a style almost diametrically opposed to the bold, forceful images of labour and struggle introduced during the Great Leap. The idea of man as an indomitable force, capable of overcoming all odds in his triumph over nature, gave way to more pensive, almost spiritual visions. Illustrations for book and magazine covers began to stress the immensity of a landscape in which the human presence played only a small role. Through broad washes of flat pastel colours, earth and sky achieved a new serenity and references to more authentic peasant traditions, patterns and dress once again found a natural integration in Chinese design.

Top, left to right: A Trip to Africa, c. 1960. Designer: Wang Rong-xian. Publisher: Writer's Publishing House. Dazai Spirit, Dazai Men, c. 1960. Publisher: Village Reading Material Publishing House. Children of God, c. 1960. Designer: Ye Ran. Publisher: Writer's Publishing House, Beijing.

Bottom left: Contemporary Albanian Short Stories, c. 1960. Designer: Zhang Shou-yi. Publisher: Writer's Publishing House, Beijing.

Echo, *1962. Designer: Zhang Shou-yi. Publisher: Writer's Publishing House, Beijing.*

回　声

李 东 春 著

周 必 忠 譯

The Future is Bright

KEXUE DAZHONG

The complete withdrawal of Soviet technicians and scientific experts in 1960 dealt the Chinese government a massive blow to its national development plans. With Soviet financial and technological assistance forming a major portion of perhaps 150 projects in various stages of completion, the severing of relations signified China's growing isolation in the world. In an attempt to project a positive and forward-looking vision of China's future, the illustrators Qin Wei, Li Zhong-yun and Wang Yong-jie introduced a series of imaginative images for the magazine *Popular Science*. Creatively rendering the inventions that would reshape China's standing in the technological and scientific world, the images also provided some nationalistic incentive for China's experts to continue independently in their research. Themes that illustrated advanced travel, undersea exploration and voyages into space were among the most popularly received, for they freed people's minds from the nation's problems while suggesting undiscovered worlds that might soon be within easy reach.

Popular Science, No. 9, 1961. Illustrator: Li Zhong-yun. Publisher: Popular Science Press. 26.0 x 18.5 cm.

Top left: Popular Science, No. 1, 1962. Illustrator: Qin Wei. Publisher: Popular Science Press. 26.0 x 18.5 cm.

Top right: Popular Science, No. 3, 1962. Illustrator: Qin Wei. Publisher: Popular Science Press. 26.0 x 18.5 cm.

Bottom left: Popular Science, No. 4, 1962. Designer: Wang Yong-jie. Publisher: Popular Science Press. 26.0 x 18.5 cm.

Bottom right: Popular Science, No. 9, 1962. Illustrator: Shen Zuo-rao. Publisher: Popular Science Press. 26.0 x 18.5 cm.

8 · The Turbulent Years

Revolution is a bitter thing, mixed with filth and blood, not so lovely or perfect as the poets think. It is eminently down-to-earth, involving many humble, tiresome tasks, not so romantic as the poets think. Of course there is destruction in a revolution, but construction is even more necessary to it; and while destruction is simple, construction is troublesome. So it is easy for all who have romantic dreams about revolution to become disillusioned on closer acquaintance, when a revolution is actually carried out.

Lu Xun, 1930

The ten years of 'The Great Proletarian Cultural Revolution' between 1966 and 1976 dramatically changed the face of China. Born out of an ideological struggle between Chairman Mao Ze-dong and President Liu Shao-qi, the Cultural Revolution gave rise to one of the world's greatest media campaigns and personality cults. From posters to plaster casts, lapel buttons to book covers, the image of Mao became synonymous with the transformation of China and the purging of what were considered to be anti-revolutionary bourgeois elements. Major demonstations were held on Beijing's Tiananmen Square for the purpose of exhibiting revolutionary zeal and devotion to the Party. Waving bright red banners and Mao's 'Little Red Book' of quotations, hundreds of thousands of youthful red guards paraded before his admiring eyes. Magazines once devoted to subjects as diverse as cooking and chemistry now uniformly featured images of the 'Great Helmsman' engaged in patriotic activities, surrounded by youthful admirers. City streets and commercial enterprises of every size all underwent name changes in an effort to display a more revolutionary spirit, and the benediction 'Long Live Chairman Mao and the Communist Party of China' was recited before every meal in even the most humble of Chinese households.

With this sudden wave of revolutionary hysteria, the aesthetic criteria for acceptable art and design once again came under tight supervision. All signs of the innovation and experimentation that had begun to show themselves in the early years of the Sixties quickly disappeared. In place of individualism, designers turned to collective production in the revolutionary realist style first developed during the Fifties.

Above: *Revolutionary alarm clock made in Beijing.*

Opposite: The Reddest Reddest Sun – Chairman Mao in Our Heart, *1968. Publisher: Zhejiang People's Art Publishing House.*

Above: *The power of the 'Little Red Book': crowds in Beijing's Tiananmen Square and* (right) *Red Guards, c. 1968.*

Learn from Lei Feng. *Illustrator: Wang Li-zi. Publisher: Shandong People's Art Publishing House.*

The recurrent propaganda themes at first tended to belie the intensity of the political struggle by continuing to reflect a concern for politics, health, construction, industry and education. Yet what separated these works from their earlier counterparts was the sudden artistic move toward hyperealistic illustration. Highly approved for its ability to portray convincingly a veritable socialist utopia, the hyperealism of this period succeeded in creating dream-like representations of the masses as an ageless and classless workforce. Posters illustrating enthusiastic brigades of workers, peasants and soldiers armed with Mao's Little Red Book were intended to show the viewer what was politically correct. In this manner the poster itself became the favoured vehicle for the transmission of party ideology. As a consequence, political posters were carefully watched by the people for any sign of policy reassessment or ideological change. This was clearly the case with the high-ranking officials Liu Shao-qi, Lin Biao and even Deng Xiao-ping, whose fall from grace was simultaneously signalled by the sudden and complete disappearance of their images from the print medium.

Through the use of large-format posters, heroic representations of workers, peasants and soldiers were spread through workplaces and schools, providing the population with instant role models for personal conduct. Many works from this period consisted of moral tales that told of brave and selfless actions by average people. In some cases entire biographies of the individuals were made public, thus creating an identifiable personality of larger-than-life proportions with which people could more easily identify. This was the case with the orphaned peasant Lei Feng who, raised and educated by the Communist Party, went on to become a soldier of extreme merit. He was elevated to the status of a hero for youthful emulation after his premature death at age 22, and

posters frequently encouraged young people to 'Learn from Lei Feng'. On several occasions entire villages were chosen as representatives of the socialist ideal. Bearing a spirit of initiative and endurance resembling that of Mao's revolutionary camp at Yan'an, communities such as Dazhai and Daqing became symbols of success in agriculture and industry.

While much of the propaganda during this ten-year period had the effect of raising individual figures of the revolution to hero status, significant attention was also given to broader segments of the population. Women's issues once again began to achieve more widespread attention. Responding to the social reforms brought about by the Communist leadership, and particularly by Jiang Qing (wife of Mao Ze-dong), women of all ages were portrayed as equals to men in tasks ranging from farming to coal mining. As Mao had once proclaimed, 'Women can hold up half the sky.' With the principle of equality achieving broad recognition and support, artists were particularly careful to avoid any suggestion of sex roles which might detract from the poster's credibility or make the slightest implication that women were somehow subservient or inferior to men. In this respect, the images of the Cultural Revolution achieved a degree of dignity and sexual equality unmatched in the earlier Western-inspired advertising, in which the notion of male superiority found perfect compatibility with deeply embedded Confucian values.

The interest given to the role of women in Chinese society in illustrations of the period was accompanied by renewed references to the folk traditions of China's many minority people. Such designs were first discovered by the artists working at the Lu Xun Academy near Yan'an, who valued them not only as a source of personal inspiration, but also saw them as embodying an indigenous and authentic Chinese spirit. During the Cultural Revolution the traditions of

Top right: *Mao Ze-dong addresses a rally at the beginning of the 'Great Proletarian Cultural Revolution', 1966.*

Top left: *Mass support for the revolution in Tiananmen Square, c.1966.*

Above: Quotations from Chairman Mao – *the 'Little Red Book', 1966. Publisher: The General Political Bureau of the People's Liberation Army of China, Beijing.*

五好花开　遍地皆春

Chinese Women (back), February 1966. The Flower of the Five Goodnesses in Blossom Everywhere. *Illustrator: Wang Xin. Publisher: Chinese Women Magazine Association, Beijing.* 25.5 x 18.0 cm.

minority painting and decorative folk-art motifs were significantly recycled as a means of enlivening party propaganda. Poster illustations often included depictions of folkloric traditions related to the harvest, as well as seasonal festivals celebrated in accordance with the lunar calendar. While the finished works were far removed from authentic folk art and minority models, the comparatively traditional drawing styles and vivid colours distinguished them from the more mundane political illustrations and made them particularly popular decorations in the home.

By the late Sixties the competition amongst Red Guards for the title of 'most revolutionary' had grown to a dangerous level, with patriotism turning into violence in many parts of the country. In an effort to quell these frequent and troublesome disturbances, Mao was forced to mobilize the army. Little reference to this or any of the other political setbacks or challenges to party authority can be sensed in the printed designs of the later part of the decade. The propaganda machine was now impervious to minor political instability and

Man's World is Mutable, Seas become Mulberry Fields – Chairman Mao inspecting the Situation of the Great Proletarian Cultural Revolution. *Poster. Illustrators: Zhejiang Academy of Workers', Peasants' and Soldiers' Arts (Zhejiang Academy of Fine Arts).*

seemingly impossible to derail. It had formed a hardened core, generating image after repetitive image showing Mao as elder statesman and in complete control of the country's destiny.

By 1970 some political posters had moved on to a more spiritual level, depicting a distinguished yet aging Mao Ze-dong immersed in reading or thought. Not until after his death in 1976 was the artistic stranglehold of the party propaganda machine broken. Yet even with the political resurrection of Deng Xiao-ping and the cautious introduction of the 'open door policy' the art and design professions were unable to make an easy recovery. The ten years of the Cultural Revolution had unleashed a violent storm which wrecked havoc on the nation and devastated the artistic and intellectual communities beyond quick repair.

The Cult of Mao Ze-dong

Far left: Journal of Overseas Affairs, *No. 10, 1959. 'Move forward under the Leadership of Comrade Mao Ze-dong and the Communist Party of China'. Illustrator: Yi Rong-sheng. Publisher: Overseas Affairs Press, Beijing. 26.0 x 18.5 cm.*

Left: Chinese Women, *February 1966. Illustrator: Zhang Fu-long. Publisher: Chinese Women Magazine Association, Beijing. 25.5 x 18.0 cm.*

The transformation of the Chinese nation into a functional work force was one of the highest priorities of the Communist leadership, and one that could only be successful through an intensive unification effort. To mobilize such a campaign meant first to recognize the numerous obstacles of class, education and geographic distribution of China's people. For Mao Ze-dong such an attempt was of crucial importance, not only for the increased economic and social changes it would bring, but more importantly, for solidifying his own political power. Throughout the ten years of the Cultural Revolution the goal of a complete and revolutionary transformation of the arts as a means of spreading 'Mao Ze-dong thought' set a precedent for the near elimination of the nation's historical traditions. In its place rose a mass campaign for the building of a national people's culture and with it the inextricable intertwining of Mao's own image as national hero.

Through the construction of enormous outdoor billboards and the printing of millions of posters, images of Mao amongst the people could be seen everywhere. Each stressed the unification of the proletariat, the strength of co-operative labour and the need to eliminate bourgeois influences from society. Even the posters themselves were now signed as collective works of art. Featuring such names as 'The Revolutionary Rebellion Liaison of China's Art Circle' or 'The Art Training Class for Workers, Peasants and Soldiers', the groups were usually guided by one or more professional artists or designers in connection with weekly classes. The effect of creating art collectively was just one more symbolic step in the attempt to destroy aspects of individualism which were at the root of China's unification problems. If the task of completing a creative work of art without the need for personal recognition could be demonstrated as successful and for the good

of the nation, then the transformation of raw labour into an unquestioning and selfless work force might also prove to be a viable possibility.

The decision to use Mao's image as a national rallying point can be seen as early as 1959 in a poster entitled 'Move forward under the leadership of Comrade Mao Ze-dong and the Communist Party of China'. Although the popular use of his image waned somewhat during the resulting debacle of the Great Leap, by 1961 it had reappeared in softly rendered images of a man concerned with improving the life of China's peasants. By 1966 the new revolutionary illustration style, which merged the techniques and philosophies of the previous twenty years, was the only visible form of artistic expression in China and quickly became associated around the world with Mao Ze-dong and the Cultural Revolution.

Right: The Great Thought of Mao Ze-dong shines with Splendour, *c. 1968. Record cover. Collective design, China Record Company.*

Below: Unite and Win a Greater Victory, *March 1971. Publisher: Shanghai People's Publishing House.*

Glory to the Workers, Peasants and Soldiers

The design and production of images to be used for domestic propaganda purposes reached enormous proportions during the years of the Cultural Revolution. In addition to the thousands of large-format posters produced for the home and workplace, additional vignettes, or small-scale illustrations, were printed and bound in booklet form to be used as models for reproduction in local newspapers, on flyers and within schools. While some of these images are only reduced and simplified versions of well-known larger works, their creation was intended as yet another reminder of the need for class struggle and 'Mao Ze-dong thought'. Despite the repetition of the revolutionary message of this period, many of the illustations are unique in that they take full advantage of their intentional small size to create more stylized and highly design-conscious emblems.

In particular, many of the marks composed of single figures are strongly developed compositions that rely on their graphic imagery to establish their geometric form. Instead of determining a diamond or circular format with the use of a strict linear border, these marks derive their strength from the graphic form of the visual components themselves. In this manner, a dynamic and cohesive effect is achieved in which an emblem uses a corner of a flag or rifle barrel to define its composition.

As all of the vignettes of this period are designed to promote Mao Ze-dong writing and thought, each illustration makes reference either to a popular quotation by Mao or to a revolutionary slogan. Through the continual representation of workers, peasants and soldiers, these small images were meant to serve as a constant reminder to the Chinese people that the revolution could only succeed through unified struggle.

Opposite, top: *Vignettes for spreading Mao Ze-dong thought, 1970. Publisher: Shanghai People's Publishing House.*

Opposite, centre and bottom: *Revolutionary vignettes, c. 1968.*

Above and right: *Revolutionary vignettes, c. 1968.*

The Model Operas

学英雄 见行动

人换思想地换装

From the beginning of the Cultural Revolution traditional theatre was branded as 'dead drama' and a 'poisonous weed' by Jiang Qing, China's self-appointed cultural tzar and wife of Mao Ze-dong. As a consequence, many respected drama troupes were disbanded, scriptwriters persecuted and performers forced to engage in demeaning labour. To replace traditional performances, a set of modern operatic works was created, answering the call for artistic expressions of revolutionary patriotism. Major productions of dance, drama and song, these model operas were performed on a continuous rotating basis with attendance mandatory for all. Each production recounted a different tale of personal sacrifice and material loss, building to a climatic confrontation between good and evil and then happily finishing with a new camaraderie between workers, soldiers and peasants.

Poster editions, based on the themes of the operas, featured the revolutionary characters rising above their earthly labours, victorious in thought and deed. Images such as these relied on the same role-model psychology as the earlier 'Learn from Lei Feng' campaign, with the added advantage that the audience could be moved by the heroic exploits played out before them and thus develop a more direct identification with the characters.

Learn from Heroes and Reflect it in one's Deeds – The People Changed their Thoughts and the Field Changed its Appearance, *October 1974. Illustrator: Hua Ting-yu. Publisher: Shanghai People's Publishing House.*

Above: *Learn from Heroes and Reflect it in one's Deeds – Put the Hardest Task on my Shoulder, 1974. Illustrator: Sun Cheng-hong. Publisher: Shanghai People's Publishing House.*

Right: *Learn from Heroes and Reflect it in one's Deeds – Learn from that Pine Tree on the Mountain Tai, 1971. Illustrators: the art training class for workers, peasants and soldiers, Shanghai School of Fine Arts. Publisher: Shanghai People's Publishing House.*

9 · Open Doors and Beyond

Writers and artists must have the freedom to choose their subject matter and method of presentation based upon artistic practice and exploration. No interference in this regard can be permitted.

Deng Xiao-ping, *Message to the Fourth National Congress of Writers and Artists*, 1979

Above: Induce Cleverness in Your Children, *1982. Poster. Designer: Wu Duan-duan.*
Opposite: The Horse Thief, *c.1986. Cinema poster. Designer: Wang Yan-lin.*

The ten years of persecution and upheaval brought by the Cultural Revolution left few people unscathed. The institutions of education and research lay in ruin and massive re-education compaigns had depleted the intellectual and artistic communities. In the years that followed, Chinese leaders began to realize the gravity and scope of the disaster and quickly proclaimed it to be the most severe error since the founding of the People's Republic. In 1978, only two years after the death of Mao Ze-dong, Deng Xiao-ping set China on a course of economic restructuring and announced his intention of pursuing an 'open door' policy. The many changes brought by the resulting economic policies held enormous significance for graphic design. The new potential for privately owned business and at least some opportunities for individual job selection brought a demand for design services, as well as the opening of careers in the design field. Nevertheless, concepts of modern communications, advertising and marketing remained virtually unknown in a country which for thirty years had only produced for centralized government distribution.

In order to understand the problems inherent in the rebuilding of Chinese design and visual communications during the Seventies, it is important to realize the immensity of China's internal and external isolation. Publishing had fallen into a serious decline during the Cultural Revolution: editors were jailed and paper was diverted for the creation of propaganda posters. Aside from radio, the communication links within the country immediately following the turbulent years were severely limited. The real use of modern mass-media techniques only came with the growth of individual television ownership during the mid-Seventies. The relatively late arrival of television was due not only to the

Above left: Shipwreck in the Indian Ocean, *1980s. Cinema poster. Designer: Hao Bing.*

Above right: The Knife destroys the Spirit, *1990. Cinema poster. Designer: Tang Yi-yong. Shanghai Film Studio.*

sustained political upheaval, but to high retail costs and limited production capabilities. For this reason it was not until the early Eighties that television was able to draw a sufficient viewing public for it to be considered a viable and effective form of communication. This latent development must be considered partly responsible for the limited exposure of the Chinese people – 80 per cent of whom live rural lives – to the concepts of mass media and advertising.

With the goal of raising China's standing in the world's export market, the small number of designers working in the late Seventies turned to any and all available sources for some clue as to how to begin. To a great extent this meant

中外装帧艺术论集

郭振华 余秉楠 章桂征编

时代文艺出版社出版

Collected Critiques on the Art of Chinese and Western Book Design, *1988. Designer: Zhang Gui-zheng. Publisher: Art and Literature Time Publishing House, Changchun.*

Top: New Translations of Tang Poems, *1987.*
Designer: Zhang Shou-yi. Publisher: People's
Literature Publishing House, Beijing.

Above: The First Cup of Bitter Wine, *1982.*
Designer: Liu Cheng-yin. Publisher: People's
Literature Publishing House, Beijing.

looking at what was now coming into China from abroad and copying it without regard for its aesthetic quality. While this practice offered limited help in orientating the design profession's approach to predominately Western markets, the unselective borrowing and mixing of visual styles and graphic forms often produced awkward hybrids. Without a deeper understanding of the intrinsic heritage and built-in cultural significance of the models they were using, Chinese designers through the early Eighties achieved only superficial results. Meantime, however, a continued relaxation of regulations governing the import of foreign periodicals and a growing interest in cultural and professional exchanges helped to prove design's potential value to leaders in Chinese business and industry.

The tremendous influx of design information also had the effect of establishing a valuable contact with Western art, music and fashion which, as a consequence, helped to stimulate a new interest in design professions amongst students. The Eighties brought new courses in graphic design to China's colleges, where important questions of form and content began to be discussed.

From an aesthetic view, many of the designs of the late Seventies seemed to return to familiar visions of the early Sixties, when Chinese design was experiencing a revival of creativity and innovation. Popular images featured Chinese landscapes rendered in broad planes of flatly brushed colour, punctuated by simple figures and symbols of rural life. Much of the commercial illustration recalled China's wealth of folk patterns and peasant traditions, with soft blues, pinks, yellows and browns making up the artist's palette. Since the advent of the Cultural Revolution in 1966 had halted any further advancement of these themes, much of the work of the late Seventies seemed to long for a lost or interrupted sense of spiritual purity and orderliness.

At the same time, the best Chinese designers realized that it was futile to move backward and sought instead a way to bring what they saw as valid Chinese motifs, graphic forms and techniques to the suddenly modern world around them. The rational order and spiritually pure styles of the Bauhaus, and later the Swiss School, were highly influential in helping Chinese designers to establish a theoretical framework for contemporary visual communication. Western acceptance of the standardized transliteration known as Pinyin during the early 1970s also presented new problems for designers. The need to give a sense of order to texts in both Chinese and the roman alphabet required a full understanding of typographic grid systems and a new sensitivity to Western letter forms.

Throughout the Eighties questions of 'external influence' continued to arise, both professionally and within China's art and design academies. Only during

汾城轶闻

——一个系统工程学家的遭遇

柯 云 路

Anecdotes in Fen City, *1987.*
Designer: Liu Quan. Publisher: Beijing
People's Publishing House.

Posters during student demonstrations, Tiananmen Square, Beijing, May 1989. The People will Win (top). The Lava is Moving, the Volcano will Erupt (bottom). *Photographer: Kosima Weber Liu.*

the later part of the decade was there a meaningful rediscovery and gradual implementation of authentic Chinese styles. A re-examination of the design theories of Lu Xun has, in part, been responsible for bringing about a recognition of the positive value of China's own design traditions.

The growing imbalance of lifestyles, education, economics and individual values has, however, raised new questions about the ability of traditional design themes to appeal to a broad cross-section of the Chinese people. The problem in forging an authentic Chinese visual language is the need simultaneously to appease the desires and expectations of China's rural people, to whom 'new' and 'Western' are often inextricably linked. Significant domestic resistance has developed toward purchasing Chinese-made products, which are seen as inferior to their foreign counterparts. To advertise, package and sell Chinese goods that do not at least bear remote resemblance to Western models, particularly in the realm of electronics, cosmetics and clothing, invites rejection.

Increasingly, Chinese designers and educators are turning to Japan as a model example of an economically advanced and technologically sophisticated

country capable of sustaining a complex cultural identity. What Chinese designers today eventually hope to achieve is a similar balance between respect for and reference to their visual past and the benefits of modernity. To a great extent China's ability to introduce and sustain the changes that will make such a co-existence possible, hinges on the political future of the nation. Yet this condition need not be as ominous as it might appear. One of the more interesting aspects of Chinese graphic design, from its initial acceptance during the May Fourth Movement to the present day, has been the clairvoyant relationship it has consistently maintained with politics. Sometimes as activist art, often a forerunner of change, Chinese graphic design during the 20th century has proved its ability to create a vision for the future while enduring the immediate conditions of its governance.

Help!, *May 1989. Painted banners. Central Academy of Drama, Beijing.*

Interpretive Illustration of the Eighties

大師和瑪格丽特

布尔加科夫著

By the mid-Eighties Chinese illustrators were once again beginning to experiment with techniques unencumbered by a concern for political correctness. The hyperrealistic techniques of the Cultural Revolution were only vague childhood memories for many of the new designers who were just joining the creative departments in the publishing industry. As a result, a number of divergent new styles were emerging which expressed the interests and influences of the younger generation.

A general preoccupation with intense colours and exaggerated contrasts in value formed a major characteristic of this period of artistic growth. In part it was the practical result of an outdated printing technology, for designers quickly learned how to turn the potential weakness of the industry to their own benefit. Unable to achieve acceptable results with the reproduction of photographs or designs that required precise registration, they instead developed approaches to illustration that exploited the aging printing process.

One of the most innovative designers, whose vision and creativity has had a major impact on the development of conceptual illustration techniques in China, is Qin Long, a Senior Art Director at the Foreign Literature Publishing House in Beijing. His book-cover designs, which develop loosely related visual narratives to the stories, reflect his early interest in Cubism and Picasso in particular. Qin's works are filled with a rich visual interplay of abstracted figures and animated symbols, demanding a degree of interpretation by the viewer. In a country whose recent history of graphic images left little to the imagination, the work of Qin Long and others has reintroduced the idea of illustrative interpretation and provided a vital link in the development of modern Chinese book design.

能干的法贝尔

马克斯·弗里施著

丰臣家的人们

司马辽太郎著

当代外国文学

Opposite: The Master and Margarita, *1988.* *Designer: Qin Long. Publisher: Foreign Literature Publishing House, Beijing.*

Above left and right: The Capable Fa Bai-er *and* Members of the Toyotomi Family, *1984. Designer: Qin Long. Publisher: Foreign Literature Publishing House, Beijing.*

西方现代派文学
问题探讨集

何慰贤 编选

国文学出版社

科尔顿中短篇小说选

当代外国文学

Far left: Research on Contemporary Western Literature, *1984. Designer: Qin Long. Publisher: People's Literature Publishing House, Beijing.*

Left: A Selection of Stories by Ke Er-dun, *1984. Designer: Yu Shao-wen. Publisher: Foreign Literature Publishing House.*

The Conceptual Image

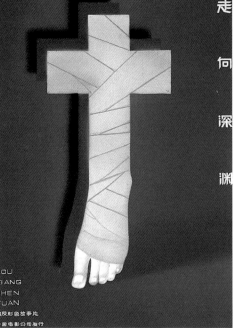

Far left and left: The Origins of Buddha *and* Heading for the Abyss, *1989. Posters. Designer: Liu Yan.*

Below: The Crisis of Our Natural Resources, *1988. Poster. Designer: Su Yun-Qian.*

Opposite: No Nuclear Threat, No Nuclear War, *1989. Poster. Designer: Liu Yi-bing.*

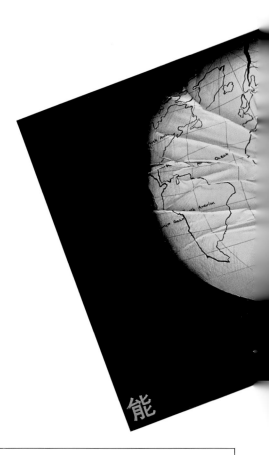

A positive effect of the Open Door Policy was a steadily growing awareness and concern for the destruction of the environment, depletion of natural resources, nuclear proliferation and religious freedom. To speak out on such themes in China, however, required a careful and articulate approach. To meet this challenge, Chinese designers turned to the creation of images that, with great visual acuity, struggled to impress on both the Chinese government and the people, the importance of these global issues.

By the late Eighties, design students and professionals were engaged in the development and refinement of a highly conceptual approach to convey such themes, as well as others which often defied literal representation. In most of the works, narrative imagery has been replaced by a high degree of symbolism, with diverse images being joined or manipulated to create new and forceful visual statements. Inspired by the unusual juxtapositions of the Surrealists, many designers have turned to the creation of similar highly metaphysical images in defiance of any strict visual logic or pictorial realism. Much of the strength of these works comes from the element of surprise as the viewer is confronted with new, often ironic pictorial relationships. The highly emotional quality of such unexpected images makes them especially appealing in a country where the predominant tendency in Post-Cultural Revolution graphic design has been a cool detachment from visual commentary. In this sense, the works that deal with domestic social or environmental problems are especially important for their willingness to confront what are seen as delicate issues in Chinese society.

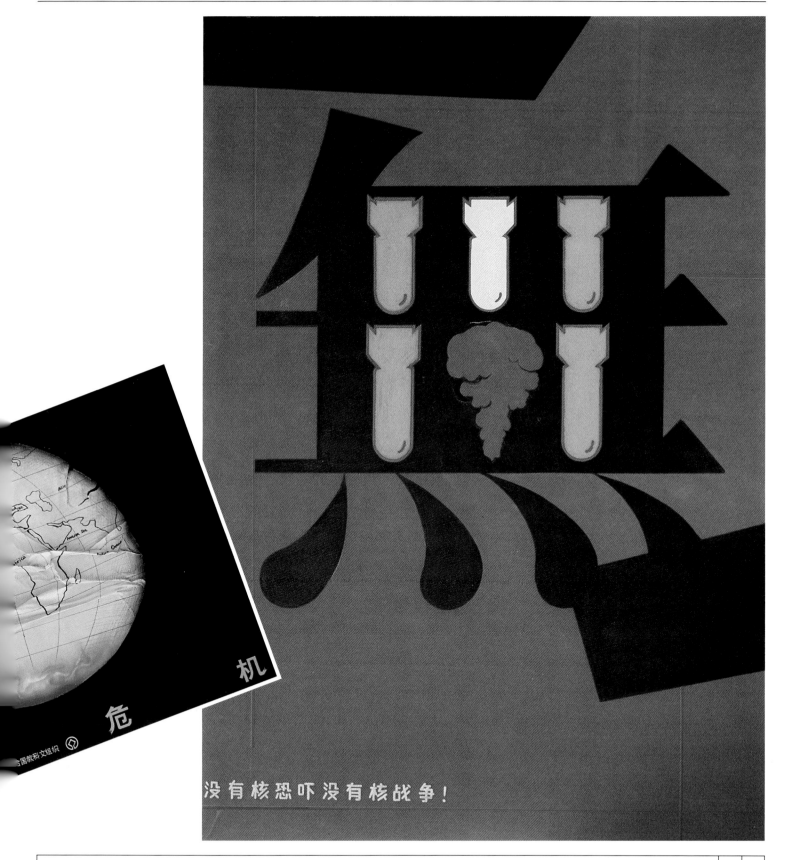

The New Wave

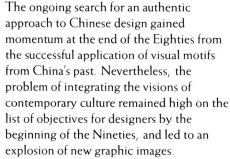

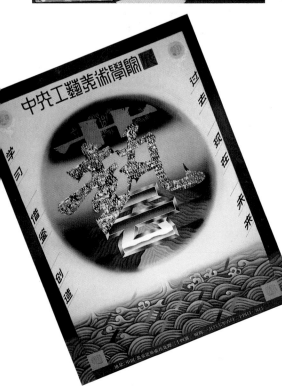

The ongoing search for an authentic approach to Chinese design gained momentum at the end of the Eighties from the successful application of visual motifs from China's past. Nevertheless, the problem of integrating the visions of contemporary culture remained high on the list of objectives for designers by the beginning of the Nineties, and led to an explosion of new graphic images.

With the cost of photographic techniques still prohibitive and computer technology for special effects out of the question for average projects, designers have increasingly turned to the medium of airbrush to achieve vibrant expressions of colour and pattern. Many designs make playful reference to elements found in classical Chinese painting or traditional architecture. Their graphic translation through the use of highly stylized lines and primary colours transcends the seriousness of the originals and achieves an often whimsical quality. In many

examples, items such as traditional kites, ceremonial masks or children's pinwheels, have taken on a new significance as pop icons of modern Chinese culture, achieving instant interest for their long ignored ingenuity.

Typography, also freed from its conservative moorings, achieves a new independence, developing a playful interaction with hand-brushed calligraphy or isolated in colourful boxes which lend a geometric order to often chaotic accumulations of symbolic images. The overall effect of these designs, despite occasional sensory saturation, is a feeling of celebration. Both liberating and evocative, such works are ample evidence that Chinese designers have succeeded in firmly establishing both practical and philosophical directions within their profession. They are not only substantial advances in visual communication, but welcome developments in a country whose design future only fifteen years ago seemed, at best, uncertain.

Opposite, top, left to right: Red Sorghum, *1987. Cinema poster. Designer: Chen Shao-hua. Best Wishes for an Abundant Year, 1988. Poster. Chimei Liquor, 1989. Designer: Gao Wei.*

Opposite bottom: Exhibition of the Central Academy of Art and Design, *1986. Poster. Designer: Zhang Lei.*

Right: A Global Spring, *1987. Poster.*

The Modern Folk Revival

Since the early part of the century, when Lu Xun first began to speak of the necessity of artists to refer continually to their enormously rich visual past, Chinese designers have struggled for a way to apply these ideas. While many attempts were made during the early years of the May Fourth Movement and again at the rebel base of Yan'an, it has not been until the late Eighties that a sufficiently well-developed application of these themes has proved successful. Political turmoil and its accompanying restrictions on art and design, as well as an understandable ambivalence toward anything that hinted of pre-industrial development, hindered a serious analysis and understanding of China's design patrimony.

With the first tastes of advanced industrial society now upon them, the Chinese have

Far left: Mountain Chrysanthemum, *1986.*
Designer: Lu Zhen-wei. Publisher: Shandong Art and
Literature Publishing House.

Left: Spirit, *1986. Designer: Lu Zhen-wei.*
Publisher: Shanghai Art and Literature Publishing
House.

Right: Sunset, *1986. Designer: Yu Shao-wen.*
Publisher: People's Literature Publising House,
Beijing.

Far right: The History of Contemporary
Chinese Schools of Short Stories, *1989.*
Designer: Liu Cheng-yin. Publisher: People's
Literature Publishing House, Beijing.

begun a slow recognition of the importance of their past. A realization of the highly expressive nature of prehistoric as well as indigenous folk arts has inspired designers in their effort to find a modern visual language unique to Chinese culture. In essence, the study and incorporation of such themes as stone engraving, woodblock and papercut have signalled a major historical evolution. The ability of a culture to express and implement a 'second-generation' self-referential design style implies an objective distancing process that, earlier, Chinese designers were unprepared or not allowed to make. The advantage that this development now holds is its unique ability to free early design influences from the confines of their original socio-cultural condition.

There are also dangers in the random application of historical styles and motifs. Although good intentioned, many designers succumbed to the arbitrary use of period images without a complete understanding of either the image or its deeper meaning. The resulting effect was too often a shallow pastiche. However, by the end of the Eighties many Chinese designers had begun to show a real concern for the question of historical interpretation and many successful folk-inspired designs of today continue to suggest their influence but show a careful regard for their contemporary context.

The last years of the Eighties also brought a revival of historically inspired typographic compositions and styles. A major development has been the reintroduction of the vertical composition of characters, which was discouraged during the previous forty

years for its intrinsically feudal implications. The use of vertical columns has fuelled interest in modern typographic styles set in the traditional format. This visual juxtaposition has given rise to many exciting designs, particularly when used in conjunction with primitive images and forms.

The revival of traditional and folk-inspired themes has offered Chinese designers a way to implement the goals of a century of searching and experimentation. The process of domestic and political acculturization to this particular phase of design may also be a lengthy one. Nevertheless, the particular beauty of the modern folk revival is its guarantee of a future of expressive variables and thereby a new ability of graphic design to speak from an intrinsically Chinese voice.

Structure and Expression

The relaxation of artistic criteria in the years immediately following the Cultural Revolution left designers with the rare opportunity to reassess the needs and desires of their profession. Their previous inability to explore fully either the interpretive or functional potentials of graphic design led to a re-awakening of these themes during the late Seventies. The designing of book and magazine covers for theoretical subjects, which often defy literal imagery, became a favourite topic for the designer Ren Yi. His meticulous studies fully explore the psychological suggestiveness of his subjects through the use of visual rhythms, symbolic colours and enlarged graphic markings. His early recognition of the value of underlying typographic systems has also been immensely influential in contemporary design; this gave harmony and order to the combined use of Chinese characters and the romanized Pinyin transliteration, without dampening the work's expressive character.

Far left: The History of the Chinese Money System through the Dynasties, *1988. Designer: Ren Yi. Publisher: Shanghai People's Publishing House.*

Left: Shanghai Literature, *No. 2, 1985. Designer: Ren Yi. Publisher: Shanghai Art and Literature Publishing House.*

Right: Aesthetic Education, *1982. Designer: Ren Yi. Publisher: Hunan People's Publishing House.*

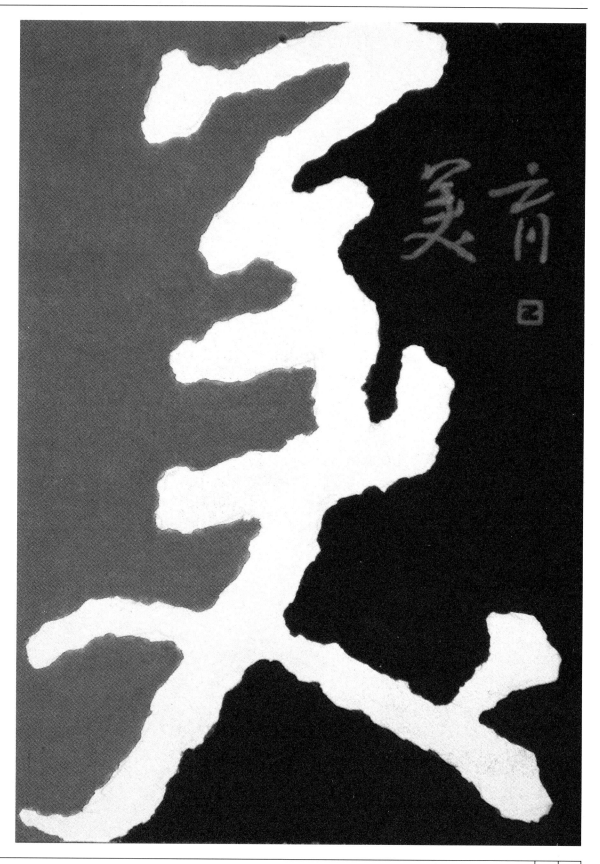

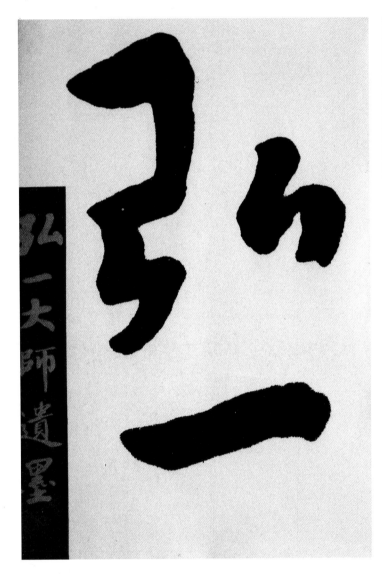

Contrasts of structure and expression are also echoed in the designs of Cao Jie. Her frequent use of large calligraphic markings, as in the book cover *The Calligraphy of Master Hong Yi*, have great graphic appeal and provide elegant counterpoints to the vertical title bars that have become her trademark. Her perception of the value of standardized graphic systems for periodicals wishing to project a consistent and identifiable image has also been widely praised.

The recent recognition of the importance both of structure and interpretive illustration has been especially helpful in the development of literary, technical and scientific publications, vital to China's drive for modernization. It is through such noticeable and concrete advances that design has had the ability to prove its worth. As Ren Yi notes, art is limited to exposure in galleries and museums. Design, on the other hand, is on the front line everyday; as a consequence, it has a special responsibility to society. Art has always been important in the ongoing development of a culture, but it is design that now has the power to educate and create meaningful change in Chinese life.

Far left: The Calligraphy of Master Hong Yi, *1987. Designer: Cao Jie. Publisher: Huaxia Publishing House.*

Left: Calligraphy Stone Carvings from the Qing and Han Dynasties, *1982. Designer: Cao Jie. Publisher: People's Fine Arts Publishing House, Beijing.*

Right: The Art of the Calligraphy of Cai Xiang, *1981. Designer: Cao Jie. Publisher: People's Fine Arts Publishing House, Beijing.*

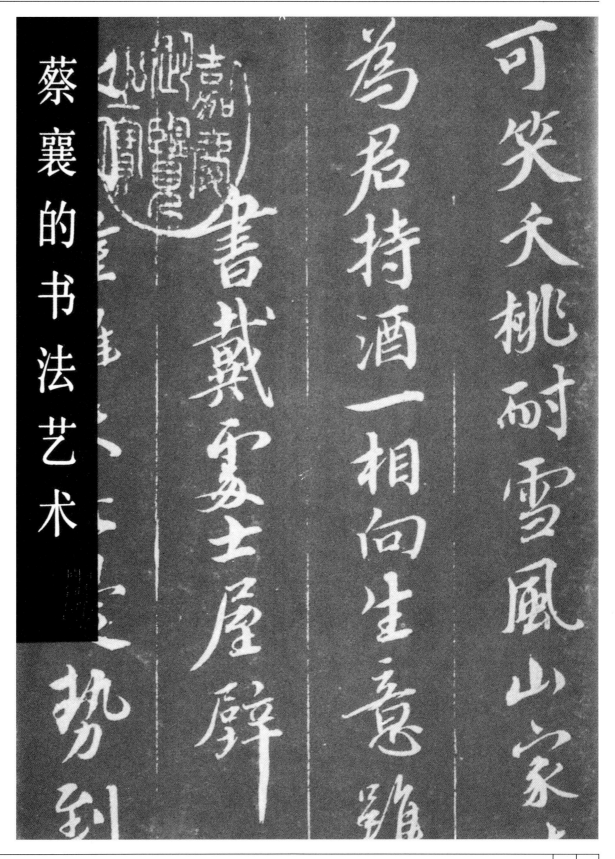

Signs of Democracy

The mass outpouring of public support through the spring of 1989 for what became known as the Pro-Democracy Movement touched all levels of Chinese life. Never in the forty years since the founding of the People's Republic in 1949 had workers, students, artists and intellectuals been united in such an enormous and spontaneous show of support for political openness and an end to official corruption. Daily demonstrations brought Beijing to a literal standstill, with hundreds of thousands of workers bearing homemade banners as encouragement for the student organizers gathered on Tiananmen Square. The square itself became a festive focal point for free expression, with a student-controlled public-address system and hundreds of makeshift placards and banners announcing the workplaces and origins of the participants. Students at Beijing's Central Academy of Fine Art

organized an ad-hoc committee to produce and distribute a variety of posters and handbills which were hung in windows and pasted to walls. Such posters were quickly produced by hand from simple woodblock techniques as they had been years before in Yan'an, with fewer than one hundred copies.

Texts for the posters were simple and direct, employing a fresh vocabulary that symbolized the vitality of an authentic people's struggle. In this sense they contrasted with the aging government slogans, which seemed cliché-ridden and out of touch with the China of today. The messages encompassed a variety of topics, from support for student hunger strikers to encouragement for journalists opposed to government censorship.

Beijing's Central Academy of Drama also played an important role in the preparation of large painted banners. Using materials

available from their scene design workshop, students painted emotional neo-expressionistic figures accompanied by large character messages pleading for help. The vivid colours and imposing size of these banners made them an appropriate backdrop for the events to follow and further extended the idea of the media stage on which human struggle is now played out.

Many of the banners and posters of the Pro-Democracy Movement also introduced bilingual texts, thus establishing a new and important link with the outside world and aiding international comprehension of this major event. Live television coverage of the Beijing demonstrations and the use by students of other electronic communication media, such as fax and telex machines, highlighted the rapidly changing nature of revolution and turned the orthodox technology of the Chinese establishment into weapons which threatened their own demise. The steady stream of images and messages emanating from China introduced a new level of credibility to the events unfolding before our eyes and the immediate and personalized nature of the fax transmissions, in particular, had a moving effect on recipients who now felt a tangible connection to a struggle taking place half-way across the world. Such forays by Chinese artists and designers into geopolitics showed the remarkable ability of design today to alter world opinion significantly. Simultaneously signalling China's emergence from a period of mass media isolation, the combined use of design and modern technology forced people around the globe to re-evaluate their roles as detached observers, by making them active participants in social and political change.

Opposite: *Painting demonstration banners, May 1989. Poster. Central Academy of Fine Arts, Beijing. Photographer: Fei Da-wei.*

Top left: The People Are With You . . . , *May 1989. Poster. Central Academy of Fine Arts, Beijing.*

Above: Give Me Back Human Rights . . . , *May 1989. Poster. Central Academy of Fine Arts, Beijing.*

Right: 1989, June 4. *Using the national emblem of China, originally designed to signify the Chinese people (four small stars) and the Communist Party (large star), to protest at the massacre in Tiananmen Square.*

Reference Guide

Chinese Publishers

	Ahead of the Times Magazine Association
方舟月刊社	The Ark Press
時代文藝出版社	Art and Literature Time Publishing House
北京北新書局	Beijing Beixin Book Company
北京人民出版社	Beijing People's Publishing House
京漢鐵路駐滬辦事	Beijing-Shanghai Railway, Shanghai Office
北京大學出版社	Beijing University Press
北京未名社	Beijing Weiming Association
中華月報社	The Central China Monthly Publishing Office
中國美術刊行社	China Art Press
中國漫畫社	China Publication
中國攝影社	Chinese Photography Association
中國婦女雜志社	Chinese Women Magazine Association
外國文學出版社	Foreign Literature Publishing House
光華書局	Guanghua Book Company
華夏出版社	Huaxia Publishing House
湖南人民出版社	Hunan People's Publishing House
獨立出版社	The Independence Press
江西人民出版社	Jiangxi People's Publishing House
良友圖書印刷有限公司	The Liang You Printing and Publishing Co., Ltd.
軍事委員會軍事雜志社	Military Magazine Association of the Military Committee
新中國婦女社	New Chinese Women Association
新工商半月刊社	New Industry and Commerce Bimonthly Press
上海亞東圖書館	The Oriental Book Company
僑務報社	Overseas Affairs Press
人民美術出版社	People's Fine Arts Publishing House
人民文學出版社	People's Literature Publishing House
科學大眾社	Popular Science Press
山東文藝出版社	Shandong Art and Literature Publishing House
山東人民藝術出版社	Shandong People's Art Publishing House
上海美術生活雜志社	Shanghai Art and Life Publications
上海文藝出版社	Shanghai Art and Literature Publishing House
上海北新書局	Shanghai Beixin Book Company
上海中華書局	Shanghai China Book Company
上海商務印書館	Shanghai Commercial Press

上海大衆出版社刊行	Shanghai Cosmopolitan Press	上海水沫書店	Shanghai Shuimo Book Store
上海創造社	Shanghai Creation Society	上海四社出版社	Shanghai Sishe Press
上海大東書局	Shanghai Dadong Book Company	上海泰東圖書局	Shanghai Taidong Book Company
上海大江書局	Shanghai Dajiang (Big River) Book Store	上海婦女雜志社	Shanghai Women's Magazine Association
上海光華書局	Shanghai Guanghua Book Company	上海嚶嚶書屋	Shanghai Yingying Book House
上海工商半月刊社	Shanghai Industry and Commerce Bimonthly Press	天津美術出版社	Tianjin Fine Arts Publishing House
上海開明書店	Shanghai Kaiming (Enlightened) Book Store	天馬書店	Tianma (Heaven Horse) Book Store
上海女子書店	Shanghai Ladies' Book Store	農村讀物出版社	Village Reading Material Publishing House
上海樂華圖書公司	Shanghai Lehua (Happy China) Book Company	人世間出版社	The World Press
上海生活書店	Shanghai Life Book Store	作家出版社	Writer's Publishing House
上海現代書局	Shanghai Modern Book Company	興中月刊社	Xing Zhong Monthly Association
上海時代圖書公司	Shanghai Modern Publications, Ltd.	浙江人民美術出版社	Zhejiang People's Art Publishing House
上海新月書店	Shanghai New Moon Book Store	震旦大學理工學院雜志社	Zhendan University College of Science and Engineering Press
上海新時代月刊社	Shanghai New Times Press		
上海人民美術出版社	Shanghai People's Fine Arts Publishing House	濁社出版社	Zhuo Press
上海人民出版社	Shanghai People's Publishing House		

Select Bibliography

Editions specified are those used by the authors

All About Shanghai. Oxford and Hong Kong: Oxford University Press, 1983.

Chan, Wing-tsit. *A Source Book in Chinese Philosophy.* Princeton, New Jersey: Princeton University Press, 1973.

Clark, Paul. *Chinese Cinema: Culture & Politics Since 1949.* Cambridge: Cambridge University Press, 1987.

Cohen, Joan Lebold, *The New Chinese Painting 1949-1986.* New York: Harry N. Abrams, 1987.

Ecke, Tseng Yu-ho, *Chinese Folk Art in American Collections: early 15th through early 20th centuries.* New York: China Institute in America, 1977.

Edgren, Sören. *Chinese Rare Books in American Collections.* New York: China Institute in America, 1985.

Feng Yuanjun. *An Outline History of Classical Chinese Literature.* Hong Kong: Joint Publishing Company, 1983.

50 ans de gravures sur bois chinoises. Maison de la culture de Grenoble, Bibliothèque Nationale, Maison de la culture de Rennes, 1981.

Han Suyin. *The Morning Deluge: Mao Tse Tung and the Chinese Revolution. Vols 1 and 2.* London and New York: Granada Publishing, 1976.

Wind in the Tower: Mao Tse Tung and the Chinese Revolution 1949-1976. St Albans, Herts: Triad/Panther Books, 1978.

Hinton, William. *Fanshen: A Documentary of Revolution in a Chinese Village.* New York: Vintage Books, 1966.

Jin Zhilin. *Aesthetic Features of Chinese Folk Art: The Good Luck Dolly.* Paris: Librairie You-Feng & Musée Kwok On, 1989.

Kristeva, Julia. *About Chinese Women.* New York and London: Marion Boyars, 1986.

Link, Perry. *Mandarin Ducks and Butterflies: Popular Fiction in Early Twentieth-Century Chinese Cities.* Berkeley and Los Angeles: University of California Press, 1981.

McDougall, Bonnie and Hu Liuyu, trans.

Literature and the Arts. Beijing: Foreign Languages Press, 1983.

Passek, Jean-Loup, ed. *Le Cinema Chinois*. Paris: Centre national d'art et de culture George Pompidou, 1985.

A Pictorial Biography of Lu Xun. Beijing: People's Fine Arts Publishing House.

Quotations From Chairman Mao Tse-Tung. Beijing: Foreign Languages Press, 1966.

Rodzinski, Witold. *The Walled Kingdom: A History of China from 2000 BC to the Present*. London: Fontana Paperbacks, 1985.

Spence, Jonathan. *The Gate of Heavenly Peace: The Chinese and Their Revolution 1895-1980*.

Middlesex, England: Penguin Books, 1982.

30 ans de photographie chinoise (1930-1960). Paris: Les Presses Universitaires de Vincennes, Paris, 1984.

Tregear, Mary. *Chinese Art*. London: Thames and Hudson, 1987.

Chinese Bibliography

Annual Book Of Chinese Publications. 中國出版年鑑 Beijing: Commercial Press, 1986.

Bi Kai-wen, ed. *Collections of Ma Da*. 馬達畫集 Tianjin: Tianjin People's Fine Arts Publishing House, 1982.

Bi Ke-guan and Huang Yuan-lin. *The History of Chinese Caricature*. 中國漫畫史 Beijing: Culture and Art Publishing House, 1986.

Cao Xin-zhi. 'After An Exhibition of Book Designs'. *Reading*.書籍裝幀優秀作品展覽觀後 讀書 Beijing: Three Association Book Store, 1981.

Catalogue. *Exhibition of Literature Book Cover Designs and Illustrations*. 文學書籍封面插 Beijing: People's Literature Publishing House, 1984.

Chinese Advertising, No. 4. 中國廣告 4 Shanghai: Chinese Advertising Press, 1989.

Chinese Advertising, No.3. 中國廣告 3 Shanghai: Chinese Advertising Press, 1987.

Ding Shou-he. *An Introduction to Periodicals of the Xinhai Period*, Vol. 5.辛亥革命時期期刊介紹 第五集 Beijing: People's Publishing House, 1987.

Dictionary of Chinese Artists, Vols 1-4. 中國藝術家辭典——現代部分第一至第四分冊 Changsha: Hunan People's Literature Publishing House, 1981, 1982, 1984.

Editor's Friends, No. 2. 編輯之友 第二期 Taiyuan: Sea of Books Publishing House, 1988.

Huang Ke. 'Periodical Designs from The Liberated Area'. *Reading* 解放區的報刊裝飾畫 讀書 Beijing: Three Association Book Store, 1980.

Huang Ke. 'Lu Xun and Book Design'. *Reading*. 魯迅聲書籍裝幀 讀書 Beijing: Three Association Book Store, 1979.

Lin Yan and Wang Yian-sheng, etc., ed. *Shop Signs of Old Beijing*. 老北京店鋪的招幌 Beijing: Bowen Book Store, 1987.

Lu Xun 1881-1936. 魯迅 Beijing: Cultural Relics Publishing House, 1976.

Lu Xun and Book Design. 魯迅與書籍裝幀 Shanghai: Shanghai People's Fine Arts Publishing House, 1981.

Mo Zhi-heng. 'An Informal Talk on the Art of Book Design'. *Reading*.書籍裝幀漫談 讀書 Beijing: Three Association Book Store, 1981.

North and East of The Big River - A Revolutionary History of the New Fourth Army during the Anti-Japanese War Period. 大江南北——新四軍抗日戰爭革命史料畫集 Shanghai: Shanghai People's Fine Arts Publishing House, 1987.

Qian Jun-tao. 錢君匋 Hong Kong: Feng Ping-shan Museum, Hong Kong University, 1988.

Qian Jun-tao. 'An Informal Talk on Book Design'. *Reading*. 書籍裝幀藝術漫談 讀書 Beijing: Three Association Book

Store, 1984.

Qiu Ling. 'Book Designer Chi Ning and his Work'. *Reading*. 書籍裝幀藝術家池寧和他的作品 讀書 Beijing: Three Association Book Store, 1982.

Selected Film Posters, No. 3. 電影宣傳畫選集 3 Beijing: Huayi Publishing House, 1988.

Selected Images of Revolutionary Model Plays. 革命樣板作品劇照選集 Beijing: Chinese Photography Publishing House, 1976.

Selections of Design: The Central Academy of Art and Design 1956-1986. 中央工藝美術學院設計作品選 Beijing: Beijing Arts and Crafts Publishing House, 1986.

The History of Publications, No. 2. 出版史料第二期 Shanghai: Shanghai People's Publishing House, 1988.

Vignettes Spreading Mao Ze-dong Thought. 毛澤東思想宣傳欄報頭資料 Shanghai: Shanghai People's Publishing House, 1970.

Wang Shu-chun. *One Hundred Chinese New Year Paintings*. 中國民間年畫百圖 Beijing: People's Fine Arts Publishing House, 1988.

Xu Bai-yi. *Practical Advertising Handbook*. 實用廣告手冊 Shanghai: Shanghai Translation Press, 1986.

Ye Lang. *Outline of Chinese Aesthetics*. 中國美學史大綱 Shanghai: Shanghai People's Publishing House, 1988.

Designer Index

Designers and artists are listed alphabetically according to their Pinyin spelling. Family names precede given names.

Ai Zhong-xin 艾中信
b. 1915 Shanghai, Jiangsu Province
While studying science at Shanghai Datong University, Ai Zhong-xin began to publish caricatures in various newspapers and magazines. Feeling dissatisfied with the prospect of a career in science, Ai moved to Nanjing to study art full-time. In 1941 his work was shown in an anti-Japanese caricature exhibition and was subsequently acquired for the permanent collection of the Central Library, Nanjing. In 1950 Ai Zhong-xin became a Professor at Beijing's Central Academy of Fine Art.

Cai Zhen-hua 蔡振華
b. 1912 Deqing, Zhejiang Province
After seeing new American illustration techniques of the Twenties, Cai Zhen-hua developed a special fondness for drawing and caricature. In 1929, he was accepted by the West Lake College of Fine Art in Hangzou, where he won a prize for his pattern designs. After graduation he moved to Shanghai, working as a graphic designer for numerous publishers, including Hongyie Advertising and Publishing Co., Xinyie Advertising and Publishing Co. and the Commercial Press. From 1945 Cai began to accept private commissions for design projects, including a collaborative bas-relief sculpture for the Chinese-Soviet Friendship Hall in Shanghai and interior designs for the Shanghai room in the Great Hall of the People, Beijing.

Cao Jie 曹潔
b. 1931 Suzhou, Jiangsu Province
Cao Jie graduated from the Suzhou Fine Arts Professional School in 1949 majoring in Chinese painting. After attending a post-graduate course in book design at The Central Institute of Art and Design, Beijing, Cao Jie became an Art Director at the People's Fine Arts Publishing House. Her book designs have received international recognition, including gold medals from the International Book Fair in Leipzig in 1959 and 1989.

Chen Ju-xian 陳菊仙
Known primarily for her Nianhua or New Year Paintings, Chen Ju-xian created many government incentive posters during the Sixties.

Chen Qing-ru 陳青如

Chen Shao-hua 陳紹華

Chen Shi-jun 陳施君

Chen Wei-zhuang 陳瑋莊

Chen Yi-fan 陳伊範

Chen Zhen 陳震

Chen Zhi-fo 陳之佛
1898-1962 Ciqi, Zhejiang Province
Having majored in machine-woven pattern design in school, Chen Zhi-fo was recommended as an overseas student and travelled to Japan to further his design studies. His acceptance at the Tokyo School of Fine Arts made him the first overseas student sponsored by the Chinese government in the field of arts and crafts. During his years in Japan, Chen spent much of his time in libraries, bookstores and museums, collecting materials on traditional Japanese crafts and the history of art. In 1924, Chen returned to China to teach at the Shanghai Eastern Art School, the Shanghai Institute of Fine Art and the Guangzhou State School of Fine Art. During this period he became very involved in the design of book and magazine covers which were largely influenced by his ongoing study of organic and architectural pattern. Chen also wrote and published many books on art and art theory, including *Pattern Composition, A Survey of Chinese Ceramic Patterns* and *A Survey of Western Art.*

Chi Ning 池寧

Fan De-kang 樊德康

Fang Yun 方勻
Known as a textile pattern designer who taught at the Hangzhou West Lake College of Fine Art during the late Twenties, Fang Yun was the only woman designer to have work selected for the cover of the innovative magazine *Contribution.*

Feng Zi-li 馮自立

Gao Kui-zhang 高奎章

Gao Wei 高葳

Gu Yuan 古元
b. 1919 Zhongshan, Guangdong Province
Gu Yuan was a student at the Lu Xun Academy in Yan'an, where he also served as an administrative assistant in a small village. His work has come to embody the popular style of the liberated areas. From 1947 to 1950 he collaborated on the journal *Dongbei Huabao* in Harbin, producing many documentary woodcuts. From 1964 Gu Yuan began a long association with the printmaking department of the Central Academy of Fine Art in Beijing. In 1980 a large retrospective was held in Beijing for his prints and watercolours.

Guo Jian-ying 郭建英

Ha Qiong-wen 哈瓊文
b. 1925 Beijing, Hebei Province
After graduating from Chongqing Central University Fine Art Department in 1949, Ha Qiong-wen taught in the Art Department of the South China PLA Military University until moving to Beijing in 1953 to work in the Military's Cultural Department. Ha gained recognition for his portrayal of military heroes during the Korean War and for subsequent work during the Cultural Revolution.

Hang Zhi-ying 杭稚英

Hao Bing 郝冰

Hong Qing 洪青
First trained as a designer in France, Hong Qing returned to China to teach design at the Shanghai Special School of Art. After the Revolution, Hong Qing practised architectural design in the western provinces.

Hua Ting-yu 華庭玉

Huang Shi-ying 黃士英
An active caricaturist on the staff of *Caricature Life* magazine, Huang Shi-ying focused primarily on war and politics. He also wrote critiques and essays on the role of caricature in contemporary society.

Ke Yang 可揚

Lang Qi 郎琦

Li Hua 李樺
b. 1907 Fanyu, Guangdong Province
A woodcut artist of exceptional ability, Li Hua focused almost entirely on scenes depicting the ravages of war and the struggles of peasants. Trained as an oil painter at the Guangzhou Art Academy, Li spent five years engaged in further study in Japan before returning to teach his newly learned wood-engraving techniques. Responsible for generating interest in woodcut throughout southern China, Li Hua was also well versed in Chinese brush and charcoal techniques. His ability to render sharp, emotive images was further illustrated in a set of twelve woodcuts simply entitled *Collection of Pictures on War.* The graphic works of Li Hua embodied the ideals of a new revolutionary art and continue to be an influential force in Chinese printmaking today.

Li Qun 力 群
b. 1912 Shanxi Province
While a student at the Institute of Fine Art in Hangzhou, Li Qun joined the printmaking group known as the Wooden Bell. In 1938 he served in the propaganda department of the Nationalist army before moving to Yan'an in 1940 to teach at the Lu Xun Academy. Li Qun was responsible for creating the newspaper *The People's Illustrated*, which circulated throughout Shanxi Province. After 1949 Li became the editor of several magazines devoted to the fine arts.

Li Xuan 李 絢

Li Zhong-yun 李仲耘
b. 1918 Ninghe, Hebei Province
Li Zhong-yun's first taste of design came when he was employed as a staff artist by the Star Printing House in Tianjin. In 1946 he began his formal studies in art at Beijing's Furen University. From 1949, Li worked in China's film industry, preparing credit titles and also as a set designer. His cover illustrations for the magazine *Popular Science* during the early Sixties were prime examples of his interest in merging documentary realism with a strong sense of imagination.

Liu Cheng-yin 柳成陰
b. 1930 Suzhou, Jiangsu Provinces
After graduating from the Suzhou Fine Art Professional School in 1950, Liu Cheng-yin joined the Art Department of the People's Literature Publishing House, where he is now an Art Director.

Liu Ji-piao 劉既漂
Liu Ji-piao served as a professor of pattern design at the West Lake College of Fine Art in Hangzhou until 1929, when he moved to Shanghai to pursue architectural design.

Liu Quan 柳 泉
b. 1956 Beijing, Hebei Province
Liu Quan majored in publication design at the Beijing Central Academy of Art and Design, thereafter becoming a graphic designer in the Art Department of the People's Literature Publishing House, Beijing.

Liu Xiao-mo 劉小沫
As a regular contributor to the early period of *The Ark*, Liu Xiao-mo designed covers and decorative title designs in a style reminiscent of Art Deco.

Liu Yan 劉 言

Liu Yi-bing 劉益兵

Lu Shao-fei 魯少飛
b. 1903 Shanghai, Jiangsu Province
At the age of 17 Lu Shao-fei published his first caricature in the newspaper *Shen Bao*. During his lifetime he was responsible for starting many satirical magazines, including *Modern Sketch*, which was the longest-running and most influential caricature magazine in China. Known for his open-mindedness, Lu accepted contributions from both young and old artists, regardless of their previous publishing experience.

Lu Xun 魯 迅
1881-1936 Shaoxing, Zhejiang Province
As China's pre-eminent reformer of literature, art and design, Lu Xun came to embody the spirit of modernism through his tenacious struggle against backward thinking and feudal practices. Using the pen as a weapon, he exposed the injustices of Chinese life during the early years of the 20th century. His personal strength and moral convictions were clearly reflected in his dedication to the May Fourth Movement and his constant encouragement to a new generation of young designers was essential in breaking down the many aesthetic conventions that had long prevented recognition of graphic design as a serious profession.

Lu Zhen-wei 陸震偉
b. 1956 Shanghai, Jiangsu Province
Lu Zhen-wei has been an Art Director for the Shanghai Literature and Art Publishing House since 1973. A graduate of the Shanghai University College of Fine Art, he had produced close to a thousand designs for magazine and book covers, several of which have won national design awards.

Luo Gu-sun 羅穀蓀

Mu Yi-long 穆一龍

Qian Da-xin 錢大昕

Qian Jun-tao 錢君匋
b. 1906 Tongxiang, Zhejiang Province
Qian Jun-tao developed an early interest in music, which remained as a major source of inspiration during his long and prolific career as a graphic designer. First exposed to design while sharing a room with Tao Yuan-qing, he began to explore the enormous potential for stylized and eventually abstract uses of line and form. By the Thirties Qian Jun-tao had become a major influence on the graphic compositions of the Progressive Movement and produced many experimental designs for the Shanghai Kaiming Book Store. Throughout the Forties and Fifties, he continued to produce many fine designs for book and magazine covers, while also beginning to exhibit his work in calligraphy and seal carving.

Qin Long 秦 龍
b. 1939 Hebei Province
A prolific illustrator and designer with a degree from the Central Academy of Art and Design, Qin Long is presently a Senior Art Director at Beijing's Foreign Literature Publishing House. His powerful and evocative book-cover designs draw heavily from traditional Chinese folk traditions while continuing to reflect their modernist context.

Qin Wei 秦 威
b. 1911 Handan, Hebei Province
Having graduated in 1935 from the Beijing University College of Fine Art Painting Department, Qin Wei became known for his early work in the Chinese film industry. Appointed as Director of the Northwest Film Studio in 1938, he designed sets and produced woodcuts for the studio's films. Following the end of the war with Japan, Qin moved to Shanghai, where he headed an underground publishing effort supported by the Xin Hua News Agency and helped to found the Shanghai Artists' and Writers' Association. From 1959 to 1960 Qin served as Professor of Art at the Central Academy of Film and began to exhibit his highly illustrative watercolours, many of which were reproduced as covers for the magazine *Popular Science*.

Ren Yi 任 意
b. 1925 Zhejiang Province
After graduating in 1948 from the Shanghai Art Training School, Ren Yi designed many book covers while serving as director of design for the Shanghai People's Publishing House between 1949 and 1966. Following the Cultural Revolution he joined the Educational Publishing Company, where he worked for ten years until becoming Vice-President of the Shanghai University College of Fine Arts.

Shen Rou-jian 沈柔堅

Shen Zuo-rao 沈左蕘

Song Xi-shan 宋錫山

Su Yun-qian 蘇蘊芊

Sun Cheng-hong 孫承宏

Sun Fu-Xi 孫福熙
1898-1962 Shaoxing, Zhejiang Province
With a background in painting, Sun Fu-xi went to Beijing in 1918, where he met Lu Xun and

participated in the May Fourth Movement. With the recommendation of the president of Beijing University, he went to France in 1920 and was accepted as an art student by the Lyon College of Fine Arts. Returning to China in 1925, he began to write and publish prose, as well as essays on art, until moving to Hangzhou where he founded the West Lake College of Fine Art. After a subsequent trip to France, Sun began the magazines *Art Air* and *Literature Tea Party*. From 1934, he travelled through China organizing art and design exhibitions, finally settling in Shaoxing in 1938, where he devoted himself to education, writing and artistic creation.

Tang Yi-yong 湯義勇

Tao Yuan-qing 陶元慶
1893-1929 Shaoxing, Zhejiang Province
Tao achieved wide recognition for his Chinese painting technique at an early age and became proficient in watercolour and oil painting in the Western style. During his career he frequently returned to traditional Chinese patterns as a source for design inspiration. With the book *Token of Depression* (1924), Tao began a long and important association with the writer Lu Xun. Among the many books on which they collaborated, *Wandering* (1929) was acclaimed as his best cover design.

Tao Yun 韜　雲

Tian Wu-zai 田無灾

Wang Li-zi 王立字

Wang Rong-xian 王榮憲

Wang Xin 王　信

Wang Yan-lin 王炎林

Wang Yi-chang 王宸昌

Wang Yong-jie 王永傑

Wang Yu-kui 王鈺愧

Weng Yi-zhi 翁逸之

Wu Da-yu 吳大羽

Wu Duan-duan 伍端端
b. 1955 Beijing, Hebei Province
After graduating from the Central Academy of Art and Design in 1982, Wu Duan-duan worked as a designer at the People's Literature Publishing House and the Foreign Literature Publishing House until moving to Paris in 1987.

Wu Hua 吳　華

Wu Yun 吳　耘
1922-77 Shanghai, Jiangsu Province
In 1940, after a year of study at the Shanghai Fine Art School, Wu moved to Wannan, south of Anhui Province, to join the New Fourth Army. He was an active caricaturist in the Liberated Areas and highly influenced by the Yan'an woodblock style.

Xu Min-zhi 徐民智

Xu Xiao-xia 許曉霞

Xu Xin 徐　新
Xu Xin graduated from the Art Department of the Beijing Film Institute. Previously a graphic designer in the Art Department of the Chinese Film Distribution Company, Xu Xin now lives in Macau doing commercial design.

Yan Zhe-xi 嚴折西

Yang Ji-ping 揚寄萍

Yang Wen-xiu 揚文秀

Ye Ran 葉　燃

Yi Rong-sheng 尹戎生

Yu Shao-wen 于紹文
b. 1939 Yantai, Shandong Province
After graduating from the Fine Art Department of Beijing Art College, Yu Shao-wen became a junior Art Director at both the People's Literature Publishing House and the Foreign Literature Publishing House.

Zhang De-rong 張德榮

Zhang Di-han 張荻寒
Zhang Di-han is known primarily for his black and white newspaper advertisements during the Thirties.

Zhang Fu-long 張福龍

Zhang Gui-zheng 章桂征

Zhang He-ming 張鶴鳴

Zhang Lei 張　磊

Zhang Ling-tao 張令濤

Zhang Qing-hong 張慶鴻

Zhang Shou-yi 張守義
b. 1930 Pingquan, Hebei Province
Zhang Shou-yi graduated from the Painting Department of the Central Academy of Fine Art in 1954. He is currently an Art Director at the People's Literature Publishing House, and a consultant for the Hunan Art Publishing House.

Zhang Xue-fu 張雪父
b. 1911 Zhenhai, Zhejiang Province
Zhang moved to Shanghai in 1929 where he enrolled in a series of night courses in the arts. In 1931 he joined the Chinese American Advertising Agency, and later Consolidated National Advertising, where he developed his speciality in the field of cosmetic packaging design. Required to produce a fresh ad. concept each week, Zhang Xue Fu found inspiration in Japanese abstraction and traditional Chinese patterning, which he admired for their freshness, simplicity and directness.

Zhao Jing-dong 趙静東

Zhao Zi-xiang 趙子祥

Zheng Ren-ze 鄭人仄

Zheng Shen-qi 鄭慎齊

Zheng Yue-bo 鄭月波
Zheng began his career as a designer during the Thirties as an advertising director for the Warrior Rubber Company. In the Forties Zhen moved to Taiwan, where he developed his skills as a painter.

Zhu Jin-lou 朱金樓
Chief editor of *China Sketch* 1935-37, Zhu Jin-lou was also an active contributor to *Saving China Caricature*.

Zhuang Ping 莊　平

General Index

Pages on which black and white illustrations appear are denoted by *standard italics*. Pages on which colour illustrations appear are denoted by **bold italics**.

abstraction, 25, 55, 60, 138
advertising, 48–51, 60, 131, 132, 136;
    earliest examples in China, 15, 18–19, 36
Agitational propaganda (Agit-prop):
    street performances, 74, *105*;
    see also mobile propaganda groups
Ai Zhong-xin, *China Sketch*, *76*
All About Shanghai, **35**
Anti-war Caricature, 75
architecture:
    references to traditional, 42, 142
    geometric decoration in, 38, 56
The Ark, **52–3**, **57**, **66**, **70–1**
Art Deco, 32, 36, 52, 56;
    in advertising, 48;
    growth of, 40;
    relation to traditional Chinese architecture, 38;
    reasons for popularity, 44
art education, 18;
    Western influence, 17–18, 21;
    following open-door policy, 134
artist associations, 39, 69, 73, 78, 108
Art Nouveau, 22–3
Art Training Class for Workers, Peasants and Soldiers, The, 124; *Learn from that Pine Tree on the Mountain Tai*, *129*

Bauhaus, 134
Beardsley, Aubrey, 78
Bi Sheng, 15
Black and White Society, The, 69
Blood and Love, 25
Bloodshed of Workers in Beijing and Shanghai, The, *75*
Book of Changes, The, 11
British and American Tobacco Company (BAT), 19

Cai Lun, 13, *13*
Cai Yuan-pei, *National Learning and Culture*, *27*

Cai Zhen-hua, *Share the Labour and Share the Fruit*, **103**
calligraphy, 12, 16, 142, 148;
    early uses in design, 25–6
Cao Jie, 148; *The Art of Calligraphy of Cai Xiang*, *149*; *The Calligraphy of Master Hong Yi*, *148*; *Calligraphy Stone Carvings from the Qing and Han Dynasties*, *148*
caricature, 74, 78
    historical use of, 78;
    in mobile propaganda teams, 74;
    see also satire
Caricature Life, 78, 78
censorship, 35, 77, 150
Central Academy of Drama, 150; *Help!*, *137*
Central Academy of Fine Art, 150; *Central China Monthly, The*, *66*, *68*; *Four Modernizations*, *113*; *Painting demonstration banners*, *150*; *The People Are With You ...*, *151*; *Give Me Back Human Rights*, *151*
Chen Ju-xian, *Father likes Work and I like Work also*, *108*
Chen Qing-ru, *Loans for agricultural construction advertisement*, *49*
Chen Shao-hua, *Red Sorghum*, **142**
Chen Shi-jun, *Stockings poster*, *49*
Chen Wei-zhuang, *River Bank*, *69*
Chen Yi-fan, *World Knowledge*, *79*
Chen Zhen, *China Sketch*, *78*
Chen Zhi-fo, 40, 42–3;
    Experience of Creation, *43*, *Literature*, **54**; *Lu Xun's Self-Selected Collection*, **42**; *Modern Student*, *38*, *42*; *Short Story Magazine, The*, *24*
Chiang Kai-shek, 73
Chi Ning, *Fashion show poster*, **50**; *South East Detective Agency poster*, *50*;
China Sketch, 75, 78, *78*, **80–1**
collectivization in art, 124
communes, agricultural, 110
Complete Collection of Buddhist Scriptures (Da Zang Jing), 15
Confucianism, 11, 84
Constructivism, 102
Contribution, **32**, *33*
Cosmopolitan, The, 76, 86, 87
Creation Monthly, **55**
Cubism, 44, 138

Cultural Associations, 78
Cultural Revolution, *see* Great Proletarian Cultural Revolution

Da Vinci, Leonardo, 38
Dada, 82
Daqing, 121
Daumier, Honoré, 78
Dazhai, 121
Dazai Spirit, Dazai Men, **113**
Deng Xiao-ping, 120, 123, 131;
    Message to the Fourth National Congress of Writers and Artists, 131
design, theoretical aspects of:
    national identity, 23, 26, 31, 40, 108, 142, 144;
    revolutionary use of, 89–93;
    social responsibility, 26, 66, 148;
    transformation of society, 77, 96, 148;
    external influence, 134
Diamond Sutra (Jin Gang Jing), 13–14, *13*
Disconsolation, **45**
Doctor Williams' Pink Pills, *18*
Duke Cai's Paper, 13
Dunhuang, 14, 40

education:
    in art, *see* art education;
    and official examination system, 35;
    reform of, 17
Einstein, Albert, 23
'Eliminate the Four Pests' Campaign, 105, *105*
Enlightened Teens, The, 98, **99**
Erosion (detail), **44**
Exposition International des Arts Décoratifs, 36;
    see also Art Deco
Expressionism, 26

Fading, **47**
Fan De-kang, *Foster the Flowers of the Nation*, **113**
Fang Yun, *Contribution*, *33*
Feng Zi-li, *Assorted Pictures from the North*, *82*
figuration, 26, 28, 138
Five Year Plan, 110
Flower Group, The, 69
Folk art, 94;
    influence on revolutionary style, 89, 102, 112;

destruction of folk traditions, 112;
    modern revivals of, 114, 134, 144–5;
    see also minority culture and papercuts
Freud, Sigmund, 23
functionalism, 62, 146;
    in graphic construction, 56

Gao Kui-zhang, *Butterfly Perfume*, *37*
Gao Wei, *Chimei Liquor*, **142**
Global Spring, A, **143**
Golden Mean, 56
Goya, Francisco José de, 78
Graphic Pictorial, *87*
Great Leap Forward, 105, 106, 108, 114, 124
Great Proletarian Cultural Revolution, 106, 107, 112, 118–129
Great Thought of Mao Ze-dong shines with Splendour, The, *125*
Gu Yuan, 96; *Autumn Harvest*, **91**; *Bombing the Bunker*, **88**; *By Comparison*, *77*; *The Lu Xun Academy of Art and Literature*, *93*; *Mediating a Marriage*, *92*; *Meeting for the Reduction of Rent*, *96*; *Teaching new Midwifery*, *96*
Guo Jian-ying, *The Woman's Pictorial*, *85*
Guomindang, 73, 78;
    and the Nationalist government, 76
Gutenberg, Johann, 16

Ha Qiong-wen, *Guarding the Peace is a Hero, Constructing the Motherland is a True Man*, *109*
Hang Zhi-ying, *Violet*, **84**
Hao Bing, *Shipwreck in the Indian Ocean*, *132*
Hausmann, Raoul, 82
He Di, 13
History of the Tang Dynasty, The (Tang shu), 14
Höch, Hanna, 82
Hong Qing, *Science and Engineering Magazine*, **64**, **65**
Hua Ting-yu, *The People Changed their Thoughts and the Field Changed its Appearance*, *128*
Huang Shi-ying, *Caricature Life*, 78

Hui Zong, 14
'Hundred Flowers' Campaign, 104

I-Ching, 11
illustration, 98;
   and fantasy, 110;
   and heroic themes, 106, 108;
   hyperrealism, 120, 138;
   and idealism, 98, 106, 112;
   interpretive, 138, 148;
   revolutionary realism and
      romanticism, 108, 119, 124

Japan:
   early influence on Chinese
      design, 40, 42;
   invasion of north-east China, 73,
      82;
   War of Resistance to Japan, 73,
      78, 92;
   contemporary influence from, 136
Jiang Qing, 121, 128
Juvenile Student, 75

Kang You-wei, 17
Ke Dao-zhong, 19
Ke Lian-hui, 19
Ke Luo, 19
Ke Ting, 19
Ke Yang, *The Enlightened Teens*, **99**
Kirchner, Ernst Ludwig, 91
Kodak Company, Eastman,
   advertisement for large-format
   camera, *58*
Kollwitz, Käthe, 26, 91
Ko Pun Beauty Soap, 19
Korean War, 102

Ladies' Journal, **84**, **85**
Ladies' Life, **67**
Ladies' Monthly, **56**, **60**
land reform, 75, 92, 96
Lang Qi, *New Chinese Women*, **106**
Lao Tzu, *Tao-te ching*, 11
Lei Feng, 120, 128; *Learn from Lei
   Feng*, *120*
Lianhui Art Association, 19
Lifebuoy Health Soap, 18
Li Hua, 96; *Down with Imperialism*, *97*;
   Struggling to Survive, *97*; *Two
   Generations*, **90**
Li Qun, 96; *Portrait of Lu Xun*, *97*;
   *Women from the Red Army helping to
   repair a Spinning Wheel*, *97*
Li Xuan, *China Sketch*, **81**
Li Zhong-yun, 107, 116; *Popular*

Science, **116**
Lin Biao, 120
Lissitzky, Lazar (El), 55
literature:
   relationship to design, 25, 30,
      102;
   themes of human destiny, 23;
   Mandarin Duck and Butterfly
      style, 44, 84;
   New Literature Movement, 44
Literature and Art Study Quarterly, *26*
Liu Cheng-yin, *The First Cup of Bitter
   Wine*, **134**; *The History of
   Contemporary Chinese Schools of
   Short Stories*, **145**; *The Song of
   Dafeng*, **106**
Liu Hai-su, 18
Liu Ji-piao, *Contribution*, **32**
Liu Quan, *Anecdotes in Fen City*, **135**
Liu Shao-qi, 119, 120
Liu Song-nian, 15
Liu Xiao-mo, *The Ark*, **52**
Liu Yan, *Heading for the Abyss*, **140**,
   The Origins of Buddha, **140**
Liu Yi-bing, *No Nuclear Threat, No
   Nuclear War*, **141**
Lou Shou, 15
Lu Shao-fei, *Modern Sketch*, 72
Lu Xun, 22, 23, 26–31, 40, 56, 78,
   91, 119, 134, 144; *Dawn
   Blossoms Plucked at Dusk*, **28**;
   Experience of Creation, **42**, **43**; *Lu
   Xun's Self-Selected Collection*, *42*,
   42; *Wandering*, **28**; *The Wild
   Grass*, **25**;
   Academy of Literature and Art
      (Luyi), 90, 96, 98;
   association with May Fourth
      Movement, 23;
   and New Literature and Design,
      26;
   and vernacular language, 23;
   on revolution, 119
Lu Zhen-wei, *Mountain
   Chrysanthemum*, **144**; *Spirit*, **144**
Luo Gu-sun, *The Material City and the
   Bankrupt Village*, 82

Mandarin Duck and Butterfly Style,
   see literature
Mao Ze-dong, 74, 89, 121–3, *121*;
   the cult of, 119, 124;
   and the Great Leap Forward, 108;

Little Red Book, 119, *121*;
   speech at the Moscow Meeting of
      Communist and Workers'
      Parties, 73;
   *Talks at the Yan'an Forum on Literature
      and Art*, 101;
   the thought of, 124, 126;
   *On the Correct Handling of
      Contradictions Among the People*,
      104
Marxism, 75, 90
Masereel, Frans, 91
mass communications and
   television, 131–2;
   see also Pro-Democracy
      Movement
May Fourth Movement, *21*, 73, 76,
   89, 101, 102, 104, 137, 144;
   relationship to new design, 22–6,
      55
Military Magazine, **73**, **77**
minority cultures, 89, 94, 112;
   revival of interest in, 98, 121–2;
   see also folk art
missionary presses, 16
mobile propaganda groups, 74, 91,
   98
Model Operas, The, 128, *128*, 129
Models for the English Alphabet, 19
modernization:
   and Soviet withdrawal, 116;
   visual representations of, 62,
      66–8, 108;
   importance of technical journals,
      148
Modern Miscellany, **68**, **84**
Modern Sketch, 78, **80**
Modern Student, *42*, **42**
Morrison, Robert, 16
Mouth of the Volcano, The, **47**
Mu Yi-long, *The Artery of Society*, 69

National Congress of Artists and
   Writers, 102
Neo-expressionism, 150
New Industry and Commerce, **110**, **111**
New Literature and Design
   Movement, 26
New Times Monthly, **64**
New Woman, 40
Ning Zong, 14

Open door policy, 123, 131
Opium Wars, 16
organicism, 22, 32, 40, 42, 52

Oriental Press, 19
Ouyang Xun, 16

paper, manufacture and varieties of,
   12–13
papercuts, 94, **94**, **95**;
   influence on revolutionary art,
      89, 96, 112;
   modern revival, 145;
   see also folk art
perspective, negation of, 57;
   planimetric space, 38
photography, 106;
   early development in China, 57;
   associations, 69;
   influence of Russian avant-garde,
      66;
   in montage, 82;
   of the Progressive Movement,
      57–9, 66–8, 70
Picasso, Pablo, 138
Pictorial Weekly, **67**
Pictures of Tilling and Weaving, 15, *15*
Popular Science, 107, 116, **116**, **117**
printing, 12–16;
   techniques of, 13;
   secular, 14;
   in twentieth century, 138;
   see also woodblock printing
Pro-Democracy Movement, 150
Progressive Movement, 40, 54–71
proletarian themes, 86;
   see also land reform

Qian Da-xin, *Guarding the Peace is a
   Hero, Constructing the Motherland is
   a True Man*, 109
Qian Jun-tao, 40–41, 62; *Ahead of the
   Times*, **61**; *Another Wife*, **40**; *The
   Big Black Wolf*, **34**; *Children's
   Music*, **41**; *The Dividing Line in
   Love*, **20**; *Going Where?*, **62**; *A
   Great Love*, **35**; *Killing Beauty*, **40**;
   Literature Weekly, **60**; *Modern
   Woman*, **61**; *The Muddy Stream*,
   62; *Shanghai Private Kaiming
   Correspondence School, Members'
   Club Quarterly*, Nos 5 and 6,
   62; *The Short Story Magazine*,
   41; *Ten Years of the Shenshi
   Telegraphic Dispatch Agency*, 62,
   63; *Xing Zhong Monthly*, **57**
Qin Long, 138; *The Capable Fa Bai-er*,
   139; *The Master and Margarita*,
   138; *Members of the Toyotomi*

Family, *139*; *Research on Contemporary Western Literature*, *139*
Qin Wei, 107, 116, *Popular Science, 107, 116, 117*
Qu Qiu-bai, 89

Rationalism, in aesthetics, 40, 64, 134
Realism, 108
Reconstruction, 106, 108; see also Socialist reconstruction
Red Army, women in, 86
reformist thinking and trends, 17, 32, 78; see also May Fourth Movement
Ren Yi, 146; *Aesthetic Education, 147; The History of the Chinese Money System through the Dynasties, 146; Shanghai Literature, 146*
Rescue China movement, 74
Revolutionary Rebellion Liaison of China's Art Circle, The, 124
Revolutions: 1925–7, 32; 1949 Liberation, 101
Rodchenko, Alexander, 66
Russian Revolution, 55

Samarkand, 12
Sakyamuni, 14
satire, 78; growth of satirical journals, 74; in photographic montage, 82; see also caricature
Self-Analysis, 47
Shanghai, 35, 74; Institute of Fine Art, 18; international concessions, 35, 78
Shanghai Industry and Commerce, 111
Shanghai Sketch, 80
Shanghai Style, 34–53, 89, 101; resurgence of, 104
Shao Jing-bang, 14
Shen Rou-jian, *Designs for paper money, 93*
Shen Zuo-rao, *Popular Science, 117*
Shi Pei-qing, *Cosmetics Poster, 48*
Silk road, 12
Situ Qiao, 40
Socialist realism, 93, 108; relationship to folk art, 102; Soviet influence, 91, 98, 102; heroic figures, 102
Socialist reconstruction, 101–8
Society for the Study of

Photography, The, 69
Sprout, 26
Students' Magazine, The, 75, 75
Su Yun-qian, *The Crisis of Our Natural Resources, 140*
Sun Cheng-hong, *Put the Hardest Task on my Shoulder, 129*
Sun Fu-xi, *The Wild Grass, 25*
Swiss School, 134
Synthetic Cubism, 38

Tang Yi-yong, *The Knife Destroys the Spirit, 132*
Taoism, 11, 13
Tao-te ching, 11
Tao Yuan-qing, 23, 23, 28–31; *Dawn Blossoms Plucked at Dusk, 29; Hometown, 29; A Jar of Wine, 31; Out of the Ivory Tower, 31; Selected Tang and Song Stories (detail), 31; Token of Depression, 30; Wandering, 30, 28; Worker, 29*
Tao Yun, *The Cosmopolitan, 86*
Television, 150
Ten Thousand Word Memorial, 17
The People Will Win, 136
Theatre: during Cultural Revolution, 128; see also Model Operas
Thousand Buddha Cave, 14
Tian Wu-zai, *China Sketch, 76*
trademarks, 15
traditional imagery, 23; as sources for inspiration, 26, 28, 31, 40, 42, 134, 136, 142, 144
Trilogy of Love, The, 46
Two Stars, 46
Two Women, 46
Typical Chinese, A, 83
typography, 14, 60, 142; early moveable, 12, 15; modern, 16; stylization and manipulation of, 39, 55, 60; development of grids and hierarchies, 56, 60, 62, 134, 146; standardization of Pinyin, 134, 146

Unite and Win a Greater Victory, 125
University Press, The, 36

Verbal Confessions, 47
Versailles peace treaty, 21
Vignettes for Spreading Mao Ze-Dong Thought, 126, 127

Wang Li-zi, *Learn from Lei Feng, 120*
Wang Rong-xian, *A Trip to Africa, 114*
Wang Xin, *The Flower of the Five Goodnesses in Blossom Everywhere, 122*
Wang Yan-lin, *The Horse Thief, 130*
Wang Yi-chang, *Cosmetics poster, 49*
Wang Yong-jie, 116; *Popular Science, 116, 117*
Wang Yu-kui, *Modern Miscellany, 68*
Weng Yi-zhi, *Guarding the Peace is a Hero, Constructing the Motherland is a True Man, 109; Go all out, aim high and achieve a complete victory, 107*
women: art and photography by, 84; changing roles of, 84, 86, 96; feudal practices, 84; representations of, 76; as targets of advertising, 36, 48, 84; during the Cultural Revolution, 121
woodblock printing, 12–15; early applications of, 13; introduction of Western techniques, 26; exhibitions, 91; modern interest in, 145, 150; popularity in Yan'an, 91, 96; as a revolutionary art form, 96, 98, 150; see also Lu Xun
World, The, 98, 98
World Knowledge, 78, 79
Wu Da-yu, *Contribution, 33*
Wu Duan-duan, *Induce Cleverness in Your Children, 131*
Wu Yun, *Designs for paper money, 93; The Enlightened Teens, 99*

Xu Min-zhi, *Fish Market poster, 51*
Xu Xiao-xia, *Newsprint Papers poster, 51*
Xu Xin, *Hai Xia, 100*

Yan'an, 86, 88–93, 96; development of artistic philosophy, 89, 96; Forum on Literature and Art, 92, 98; break with Shanghai design traditions, 101–2
Yan Zhe-xi, *Shanghai Sketch, 80*
Yan Zhen-qing, 16
Yang Ji-ping, *New Chinese Women, 106*

Yang Wen-xiu, *Guarding the Peace is a Hero, Constructing the Motherland is a True Man, 109*
Ye Ran, *Children of God, 114*
Yi Rong-sheng, *Move Forward Under the Leadership of Comrade Mao Ze-dong and the Communist Party of China, 124*
Yin and Yang principle, 11
Yu Shao-wen, *A Selection of Stories by Ke Er-dun, 139; Sunset, 145*
Yuan Shi-kai, 74

Zhang De-rong, *Art and Life Magazine, 38*
Zhang Di-han, *My Dear Cigarettes, 18*
Zhang Fu-long, *Chinese Women, 124*
Zhang Gui-zheng, *Collected Critiques on the Art of Chinese and Western Book Design, 133*
Zhang He-ming, *The Flowers of the Great Leap, 112*
Zhang Lei, *Exhibition of the Central Academy of Art and Design, 142*
Zhang Ling-tao, *The Ladies' Journal, 24*
Zhang Qing-hong, 48, *Watches and clocks advertisement, 49*
Zhang Shou-yi; *Contemporary Albanian Short Stories, 114; Echo, 115; New Translations of Tang Poems, 134*
Zhang Tu-xin, 15
Zhang Xue-fu, *New literature advertisement, 60*
Zhao Jing-dong, *A Peasant Woman Yesterday: A Productive Expert Today, 108*
Zhao Zi-xiang, *Cigars advertisement, 49; Silk umbrellas poster, 50; Watches and clocks poster, 49*
Zhejiang Academy of Workers', Peasants' and Soldiers' Arts, *Man's World is Mutable, 123*
Zheng Ren-ze, illustration for a book cover, *39*
Zheng Shen-qi, *The World of Youth, 75, 75*
Zheng Yue-bo, advertisement for Mirror Box, *58*
Zhou En-lai, 107
Zhou Yang, 106
Zhu Jin-lou, *China Sketch, 80*
Zhuang Ping, *The Flowers of the Great Leap, 112*